NEED to KNOW

Edexcel A-LEVEL POLITICS

Toby Cooper

HODDER EDUCATION
AN HACHETTE UK COMPANY

Hachette UK's policy is to use papers that are natural, renewable and recyclable products and made from wood grown in sustainable forests. The logging and manufacturing processes are expected to conform to the environmental regulations of the country of origin.

Orders: please contact Bookpoint Ltd, 130 Park Drive, Milton Park, Abingdon, Oxon OX14 4SE. Telephone: (44) 01235 827827. Fax: (44) 01235 400401. Email: education@bookpoint.co.uk

Lines are open from 9 a.m. to 5 p.m., Monday to Saturday, with a 24-hour message answering service. You can also order through our website: www.hoddereducation.co.uk

ISBN: 978 1 5104 2853 9

© Toby Cooper

First published in 2018 by
Hodder Education,
An Hachette UK Company
Carmelite House
50 Victoria Embankment
London EC4Y 0DZ

Impression number   10 9 8 7 6 5 4 3

Year   2022 2021 2020 2019

Typeset in India by Aptara

Printed in India

A catalogue record for this title is available from the British Library.

Contents

Getting the most from this book

This *Need to Know* guide is designed to help you throughout your course as a companion to your learning and a revision aid in the months or weeks leading up to the final exams.

The following features in each section will help you get the most from the book.

You need to know

Each topic begins with a list summarising what you 'need to know' in this topic for the exam.

Exam tip

Key knowledge you need to demonstrate in the exam, tips on exam technique, common misconceptions to avoid and important things to remember.

Key terms

Definitions of highlighted terms in the text to make sure you know the essential terminology for your subject.

Synoptic links

Reminders of how knowledge and skills from different topics in your A-level relate to one another.

Do you know?

Questions at the end of each topic to test you on some of its key points. Check your answers here: www.hoddereducation.co.uk/needtoknow/answers

End of section questions

Questions at the end of each main section of the book to test your knowledge of the specification area covered. Check your answers here: www.hoddereducation.co.uk/needtoknow/answers

1 UK politics

1.1 Democracy

You need to know

- democracy means rule by the people
- democracy can be direct or indirect
- franchise and suffrage mean the right to vote
- who can vote has changed
- pressure groups seek to influence government, both promoting and harming democracy
- rights are essential in a democracy
- that there have been conflicts over rights

Representative and direct democracy

Features of democracy

Democracy is:

- rule by the people
- it can be direct or indirect

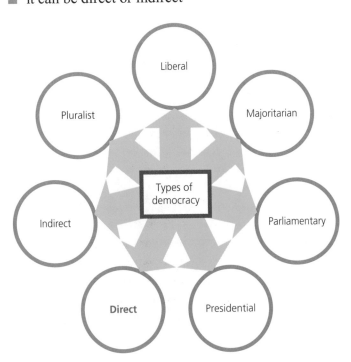

Key term

Direct democracy When decisions are made directly by the people.

Exam tip

Different types of democracy will result in different outcomes; this is not the same as being 'undemocratic'.

Functions of democracy include:

- representation
- accountability
- participation
- power dispersal
- legitimacy
- education

Direct and representative democracy

The UK is a **representative democracy** with some direct elements:

- Direct elements include referendums, petitions, citizens' juries and public consultations.
- Representative elements include elections, Parliament and devolved bodies.

Direct democracy

Table 1 **Advantages and disadvantages of direct democracy**

Advantages	Disadvantages
A purer form of democracy	Not practical
Greater legitimacy to a decision	Leads to tyranny of the majority
Improves political participation	Undermines elected representatives
Increases public engagement	Can be low turnout
Educates the public	People do not understand the issues
It works	People decide emotionally

Representative democracy

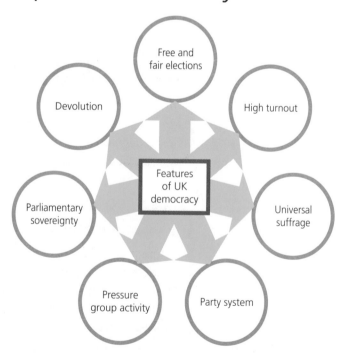

Exam tip

Remember the functions of democracy by the acronym RAPPLE.

Key terms

Representative democracy When the people elect a representative to make decisions on their behalf.

Legitimacy The legal right to make decisions and take action.

Synoptic links

Referendums are the most common form of direct democracy; arguments about referendums apply to direct democracy.

In the USA, initiatives are used, which are like referendums but are initiated by the people, not the government.

Synoptic link

Elections are fundamental to a representative democracy, but different electoral systems can have very different results.

Table 2 Evaluation of representative democracy in the UK

Element	Positive	Negative
Elections	Regular elections	The monarch and Lords are not elected
Turnout	Increasing since 2001 in general elections	Other elections usually below 50%
Universal suffrage	Everyone over 18 with few exceptions can vote	Case for 16 and 17-year olds to vote, prisoners cannot vote, homeless are often excluded
Party system	UK has a multi-party system	Safe seats and two-party dominance
Pressure groups	Campaign for and protect minority interests	Act in own self-interest rather than national good
Parliamentary sovereignty	Parliament has power to control the government	Parliament is usually dominated by the government
Devolution	Spreads power to local communities	Has created an imbalance in the UK system; the West Lothian question

Reforming UK democracy

Problems with UK democracy could be solved by reforming the system.

Table 3 Assessment of potential democratic reforms

Reform	Positive	Negative
Electoral reform	Proportional/fairer results	Confusing; lack of clear mandate
Compulsory voting	Increased turnout	Ill-informed voting
Elected Lords	More democratic	Potential gridlock
English devolution	Solves West Lothian question	Undermines Parliament/UK
Online voting	Increased/easier turnout	Fear of hacking/corruption
Codifying the constitution	Limit the power of the government	Increase the power of the judiciary
State funding for parties	Fairer competition	Extremist parties get public money

Exam tip

Consider the aim of each reform and why it might be needed.

Do you know?

1 What are the main types of democracy?
2 What is the role of direct democracy in the UK political system?
3 Why is democracy important?
4 How does representative democracy operate in the UK?
5 What are the problems with UK democracy?
6 How and why should UK democracy be reformed?

Key term

Mandate The legitimacy given to carry out manifesto promises, usually through elections.

Synoptic link

Democratic reforms in the UK would also be constitutional reforms.

1.2 Participation

You need to know

- how the franchise has been extended
- about campaigns to extend the franchise
- ways in which people can participate
- arguments for and against a participation crisis in the UK

Extension of the franchise

Who has **the franchise** is important because:

- Those who can vote decide who will run the country.
- Those who have **suffrage** can vote for their own interests.
- Politicians can ignore those without the franchise.
- People who contribute to the state (paying taxes or military service) should have a say in how it is run.

The franchise was extended many times between 1832 and 1969, shown in Table 4.

Table 4 **The extension of the franchise**

Reform	Who could vote
The Great Reform Act, 1832	Property owners/wealthy renters
The Representation of the People Act, 1918	All men 21+
	Married women 30+
The Equal Franchise Act, 1928	All men and women 21+
The Representation of the People Act, 1969	All men and women 18+

Modern campaigns to extend the franchise

Groups barred from voting:

- under 18s
- prisoners
- those sectioned
- lords and monarch

Key terms

The franchise Who has the right to vote.

Suffrage The right to vote.

Synoptic link

Lowering the voting age to 16 is supported by the Labour Party, Green Party, SNP and Liberal Democrats and has happened in the Scottish Parliament and Welsh Assembly.

The 'Votes at 16' campaign aims to extend the franchise to 16-year-olds because they believe that they will be:

■ engaged   ■ empowered   ■ inspired

Methods used by the campaign include:

■ adopting a Lord (to petition)
■ a draft document to send to your MP
■ advice on raising awareness, through its website and promotional literature
■ encouraging debate and discussion

By giving 16-year-olds the right to vote, problems relating to a **democratic deficit** may be alleviated.

Participation

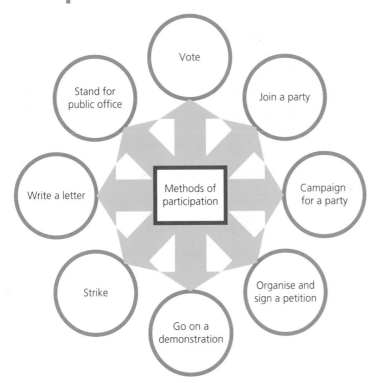

Is there a participation crisis?

Yes	No
■ Falling turnout ■ Decline in party membership ■ End of corporatism	■ Increased turnout since 2001 ■ More parties ■ Labour membership has increased ■ Increased pressure group membership ■ Rise of social campaigns

Do you know?

1 Who currently has the franchise and who is excluded?
2 How and why was the franchise extended?
3 What methods has the campaign for Votes at 16 used?
4 What are the main methods of participating in politics in the UK?
5 Why is participation important?
6 Why can the UK be said to be experiencing a participation crisis?
7 What is the evidence to suggest that the UK is not suffering from a participation crisis?

1.3 Pressure groups

You need to know
- what a pressure group is
- different types of groups
- pressure group methods
- other types of groups

Types of group

Key **pressure group** distinctions:
- **sectional** vs **causal**
- insider vs outsider

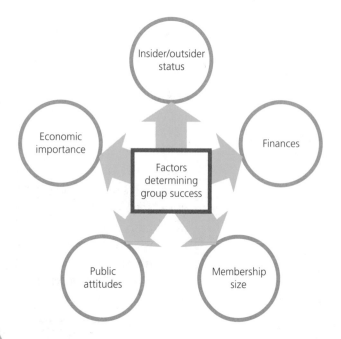

Synoptic link

Participation in elections is closely related to voting patterns and trends across elections.

Key terms

Pressure groups Organisations that attempt to put pressure on those in power to achieve their aims.

Sectional groups Groups that campaign for their own interests.

Causal groups Groups that campaign for a cause on behalf of others.

Exam tips

- None of the group distinctions are perfect and many groups have elements of both: the British Medical Association (BMA) will promote public health issues (causal) but also campaign for the interests of doctors (sectional).
- Insider/outsider status of pressure groups can change depending on the government.

Synoptic link

Pressure groups are often compared and related to particular parties; the distinction between a party and pressure group can be blurred.

Pressure group methods:

- demonstrations
- publicity campaigns
- strike
- test cases
- civil disobedience
- publicity stunts
- force the government lobbying

Table 6 **Pressure group case studies**

Group	Successes	Lack of success
BMA	Lobbying the government to ban work place smoking	Preventing the establishment of a '7 day' NHS
End Female Genital Mutilation (FGM) European network	Persuading governments to enact laws against FGM	Creating unified European strategy

Other types of groups

Think tanks:

- develop policy ideas
- research key areas
- promote a sectional agenda

Lobbyists:

- are groups with personal connections to those in power
- are hired by other groups to gain access to those in power
- seek to persuade those in power on behalf of other people (who pay)

Corporations:

- are big businesses and financial organisations
- control an important sector of the economy
- seek favourable legislation and government action
- can threaten to relocate to pressure the government

Exam tip

Being unsuccessful and failing are not necessarily the same thing; unsuccessful can mean an aim is not yet achieved; failure means the aim cannot be achieved.

Key terms

Think tanks Groups that are privately funded to research and develop policy ideas.

Lobbyists People hired to persuade those in power.

Do you know?

1 What are the key classifications of pressure groups?
2 What is the purpose of groups in a democracy?
3 Why do different pressure groups adopt different methods?
4 How have two pressure groups had success and limited success?
5 What do lobbyists, think tanks and corporations do?

Synoptic link

Think tanks have replaced the party function of policy formulation in recent years.

1.4 Rights in context

Civil rights and liberties

Human rights are absolute, universal and fundamental.

■ positive rights = clearly set out in law
■ negative rights = not illegal

The Human Rights Act (1998) changed negative rights into positive rights.

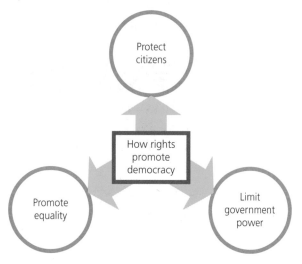

Key terms

Civil rights Freedom to do something.

Civil liberties Freedom from the government.

Synoptic link

The Human Rights Act is a key part of the UK constitution and regulates the relationship between the different branches of government.

Civic responsibilities

Legal responsibilities	Social responsibilities
■ Obey the law ■ Pay taxes ■ Respect others ■ Performing public service	■ Voting ■ Taking care of yourself ■ Taking care of your environment

Rights conflicts

■ Rights are upheld by the **judiciary** and the government.
■ There are conflicts between the government and the senior judges over which rights are protected and how.

Key terms

Civic responsibilities Duties a citizen is expected to perform. They can be legal or social.

Judiciary The judiciary refers to the judges in the UK. In political terms it specifically means the senior judges who interpret the law.

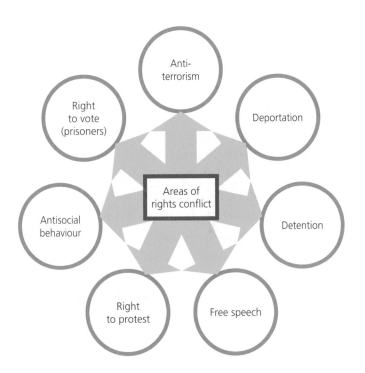

Synoptic link

Rights conflicts have risen as judicial power has evolved; see section 2 on the Supreme Court.

Rights protection

Are judges or Parliament better at protecting rights?

Table 7 Judicial vs parliamentary protection

Judicial		Parliamentary	
Strengths	**Weaknesses**	**Strengths**	**Weaknesses**
Power of judicial review	Lacks power to enforce	Parliamentary sovereignty	Parliament dominated by government
Legal expertise	Unaccountable	Passes/amends Acts	Can suspend Human Rights Act (HRA)
Independence	Works with government	Representative	Political
Neutrality	Unrepresentative	Accountable	Populist

Synoptic link

Liberties are often protections from the government, but the government and Parliament are supposed to defend civil rights.

Do you know?

1 What are the key types of rights in the UK?
2 Why are rights important in a democracy?
3 How are rights protected in the UK?
4 Why has there been conflict between the government and judiciary over rights?

Exam tip

You should be able to explain why each strength is a strength and each weakness is a weakness.

1.5 Political parties

Features of parties

Features of **political parties**:

■ range of interests
■ contest elections to win
■ seek to gain power
■ internally democratic
■ regulated by the Electoral Commission
■ have members with similar backgrounds

Functions of parties

Parties play an important role in representative democracies. They contest elections, turn general ideas into clear policy proposals through publishing a manifesto, hold governments to account and provide a link between the people and those in power.

Table 8 **Party functions and activities**

Functions	Activities
■ Representation of members ■ Participation in party activities ■ Education of the public ■ Recruitment of candidates for office ■ Policy formulation ■ Sustaining government ■ Scrutinising government	■ Canvassing ■ Delivering leaflets ■ Fundraising dinners ■ Selecting candidates ■ Local party meetings ■ 'Get out the vote' activities ■ Organising conferences

Party systems

Table 9 **Different party systems**

Single-party	Only one party exists and has total control
Dominant party	One party dominates the system, though others exist
Two-party	Two parties have a chance of gaining power
Two-and-a-half-party	Two main parties and a significant minor party which will act as 'king-maker'
Multi-party	Many parties have a chance of gaining power through coalitions

Key term

Political parties Groups of people with similar beliefs, which promote ideas and/or causes that are important to their members.

Synoptic link

Parties play an important role in promoting democracy in the UK and can be contrasted with pressure groups.

Exam tip

Although the UK is often seen as a two-party system, it is important to understand how it can be described differently and that different parts of the UK have different party systems.

Party funding

To contest elections and fulfil their other functions, parties require funds. Usually this comes from private sources, such as membership fees and wealthy donors or groups, but these sources have been declining since the 1970s. Since then, the introduction of **short money** and **Cranborne money** have given some limited form of **state party funding** to opposition parties to help them hold the government to account.

Controversies in the late 1990s and early 2000s over where party money was coming from led to two new regulations:

- Political Parties, Elections and Referendums Act, 2000
- Political Parties and Elections Act, 2009

Plans to introduce full state funding are controversial and keenly debated as shown in Table 10.

Table 10 Arguments for and against the state funding of parties

For	Against
It would reduce the influence of wealthy individuals and groups.	Taxpayer money should not be spent funding party activities.
It might improve the image of politics by making it appear less corrupt.	It might increase perception of corruption if taxpayer money is misspent.
It would allow parties to compete on a more equal basis.	Parties will remain unequal depending on membership size and other factors.
It could be used to promote smaller parties outside of Westminster.	People may object to taxpayer money being given to fund extremist parties.
It would reduce the need for politicians to waste time raising funds.	Many fundraising activities involve democratic participation.

Do you know?

1 What is a political party?

2 Why are parties important in a democracy?

3 What do political parties do?

4 What are the different party systems?

5 What reforms have been introduced to party funding since 2000?

6 What are the arguments for and against state funding of parties?

Synoptic link

The success of parties and the nature of the party system often comes down to how parties are perceived through their portrayal in the media.

Key terms

Party system Political system comprising a number of parties that competitively contest elections.

Short money State funds given to opposition parties in the House of Commons to cover costs and help fund scrutiny of the government.

Cranborne money State funds for opposition parties in the House of Lords.

State party funding Money given to political parties to cover their costs from the taxpayer.

Synoptic link

Attempts to limit party spending and funding in the USA have been limited by constitutional rulings that they undermine free speech and free expression, leading to American elections costing billions, while UK elections are in the millions.

1.6 UK political parties

You need to know

- the differences between left wing and right wing
- the differences between and within parties
- what social democracy means
- different types of parties that operate in the UK
- the key policies and ideals of the established parties in the UK

Classifying parties in the UK

Table 11 UK party types

Mainstream	Nationalist	Single-issue
<ul><li>Conservatives</li><li>Labour</li><li>Liberal Democrats (originally the Liberal Party)</li></ul>	<ul><li>SNP</li><li>Plaid Cymru</li><li>Mebyon Kernow</li><li>British Democratic Party</li><li>English Democrats</li></ul>	<ul><li>UKIP</li><li>Green Party</li><li>Christian Democratic Party</li></ul>

Parties can also be classified by where they sit on the **political spectrum** between the **left wing** and **right wing**.

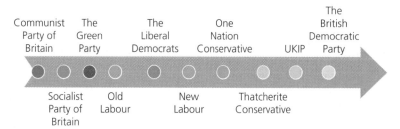

Figure 1 The British political spectrum

The mainstream parties

The Conservative party

The two main schools of thought in the Conservative Party are:

- **One nation:** Conservative ideology that believes society should provide support to ensure the gap between rich and poor is not substantial.
- **Thatcherite:** neo-liberal ideology that promotes the role of the individual and reduces the role of the state.

Key terms

Mainstream parties Those parties that have been prominent for over 100 years and seek to represent the whole UK across many issues.

Nationalist parties Parties representing a nationalist identity and agenda based on regional and cultural cause.

Single-issue parties Parties that have one driving ideological cause that informs all other policy decisions.

Political spectrum A left–right spectrum that is based on a belief in the role of government and economic principles.

Left wing Those who tend to favour greater government involvement and a regulated economy.

Right wing Those who tend to believe in a smaller role for the government and a less regulated economy.

Table 12 Key Conservative policies in 2017

Policy area	One nation	Thatcherite
Economy	■ Expand apprenticeships ■ Cap on energy prices	■ Raising the personal tax allowance ■ No rise in taxation, VAT or National Insurance ■ Private funding of social care
Home affairs	■ A law on 'victim's rights' ■ Commitments to protect EU residents already in the UK	■ Limit immigration ■ 'The snooper's charter'
Health	■ Increase NHS spending	■ Integrate health and social care
Education	■ Increase grammar schools ■ Protect school funding per pupil	■ Continue supporting privately funded academies
Foreign affairs	■ Remain in the single market	■ Leave the EU

The Labour party

The two main schools of thought in the Labour party revolve around the ideas of:

- **Social democracy:** a form of socialism that operates within a capitalist system where the government promotes wealth redistribution to provide for greater social equality, commonly associated with Old Labour.
- **Third way** or **Blue Labour:** a compromise between Old Labour social democracy and Thatcherite neo-liberalism; it is pragmatic and promotes individualism within a social framework.

Synoptic link

Despite a party's name, it may not consistently follow an ideology; the Conservative party can be described as being liberal on economic matters.

Table 13 Key Labour policies in 2017

Policy area	Old Labour	New/Blue Labour
Economy	■ Increase minimum wage ■ Reintroduce a higher top rate of tax	■ Cut the deficit and balance the economy ■ No rise in VAT, National Insurance or income tax
Home affairs	■ Cap on non-EU workers ■ Restrict immigration ■ Scrap police crime commissioners	■ Establish a victim's law
Health	■ Additional funding for the NHS	■ Limit the profit private firms can make from the NHS
Education	■ Scrap university tuition fees ■ End charitable status of private schools	■ Create privately funded academies and expand them
Foreign affairs	■ Support Brexit	■ Support for a softer Brexit retaining the single market

The Liberal Democrats

The two main schools of thought in the Liberal Democrats are:
- **Classical liberalism:** a liberal ideology that promotes personal liberty and a limited role for the government in economic matters, associated with the Orange Book group.

■ **Social liberalism:** a type of liberalism that focuses on individual rights and liberties for the individual that will ensure protection for all through government intervention to promote tolerance and equality.

Table 14 Key Liberal Democrat policies in 2017

Policy area	Orange Book	Social liberals
Economy	■ Deal with the deficit through a mixture of cuts and tax rises	■ Introduce a 1p tax increase to fund the NHS
Home affairs	■ New claimants to attend English language course before receiving Job Seeker's allowance	■ End imprisonment for drugs for personal use
Health	■ Integrate health and social care budgets	■ Increase NHS spending
Education	■ Maintain university tuition fees	■ A core curriculum including sex education
Foreign affairs	■ End nuclear deterrent ■ Remain in the single market	■ End nuclear deterrent ■ Remain in the EU

Do you know?

1 What are the differences between left-wing and right-wing ideas?

2 How can the main political parties be classified?

3 How do the main parties relate to ideologies?

4 How are the main parties structured?

5 What divisions exist within the main parties?

1.7 UK electoral systems

You need to know

■ the purpose of elections

■ the different types of electoral systems

■ the workings of FPTP, SV, STV and AMS

■ the advantages and disadvantages of each electoral system

■ why different electoral systems are used for different elections

■ the impact different electoral systems have had

■ how different electoral systems affect party representation

Key term

Democratic legitimacy
The consent of the people to be governed by the government, usually through elections.

Elections play a vital role in democracies as they bestow **democratic legitimacy** on those elected to power as well as providing opportunities for representation and participation.

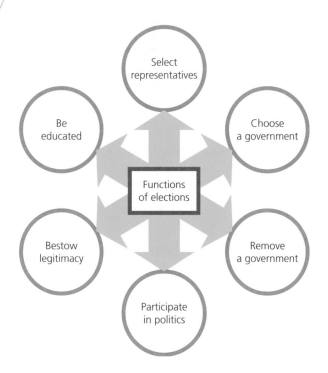

Synoptic links

To be democratic, elections should be free and fair.

Rights of free speech and press help to make elections free, while the principle of one person one vote and equal-sized constituencies are designed to make elections fair.

Table 15 Types of electoral systems

Type	Description	Example
Plurality	A candidate only needs one more vote than anyone else.	FPTP
Majoritarian	Candidates are expected to achieve a majority of the votes (50%+1).	SV
Proportional representation	Votes are allocated on a proportional basis across large multi-member constituencies.	STV
Hybrid systems	Any system that combines a mixture of two other types of system.	AMS

First past the post (FPTP)

The main voting system of the UK, FPTP, is a plurality system that requires only one more vote than anyone else to win a seat. Most issues of electoral reform concern the effects of FPTP on representation in Westminster.

Table 16 Workings of FPTP

Type	Plurality
Constituency size	Small, single member
Number of votes per person	One vote per person (as an X)
Voting for	A single candidate
Description	Within the constituency whoever has the most votes becomes the single representative for the whole constituency
Where used	UK general elections, most local council elections in England

FPTP tends to:

- benefit large parties with concentrated support
- lead to **safe seats**
- result in a few key **marginal seats**
- lead to a number of **minority seats**
- promote a two-party political system
- benefit smaller parties with concentrated geographical support
- result in single-party government
- disadvantage smaller parties with widespread support
- result in a winner's bonus where parties win many seats by small margins

Table 17 **Advantages and disadvantages of FPTP**

Advantages of FPTP	Disadvantages of FPTP
- Simple - Traditional - Clear constituency result - Strong and stable government - Government accountability - Clear MP–constituency link - Excludes extremist fringe parties	- Little choice - Minority representatives - Votes are of unequal value - Elective dictatorship - Does not always lead to single-party majority (2010 and 2017) - Unrepresentative governments - Disproportional outcomes - Excludes smaller parties

Supplementary vote (SV)

Table 18 **The workings of SV**

Type	Majoritarian
Constituency size	Small, single member
Number of votes per person	Two votes on a preferential basis (first choice and second choice)
Voting for	A single candidate
Description	If a candidate gains 50%+1 of the first-choice votes, they are elected. If not, all but the top two candidates are eliminated and the second-choice votes are redistributed to the top two candidates (if they were the second choice)
Where used	London and other elected mayors in England and the PCCs

Table 19 **Advantages and disadvantages of SV**

Advantages of SV	Disadvantages of SV
- It makes it more likely that a candidate has majority support. - It provides voters with more choice as they have two votes. - Voters can show support for smaller parties and still choose a likely winner. - To win, a candidate would require broad support. - It would retain a strong MP–constituency link.	- The winning candidate is not guaranteed to get 50% of the total votes cast. - It makes it possible for the second-placed candidate to win. - It does not benefit smaller parties in a practical sense. - There will still be many wasted votes. - It is likely to promote more of a two-party system and be less representative than FPTP.

Key terms

Safe seats Seats that remain loyal to one party and are unlikely to switch allegiance.

Marginal seats Seats that are competitive and can be won narrowly, with more than one party having a chance to win it.

Minority seats Seats in which candidates are elected by a minority of the electorate (less than half)

Exam tip

FPTP is the current Westminster system, so questions about reform will require a comparison of FPTP with other systems. Make sure you relate the arguments around FPTP to the other systems.

Single transferable vote (STV)

Table 20 The workings of STV

Type	Proportional
Constituency size	Large multi-member (6–8)
Number of votes per person	As many votes as there are candidates
Voting for	Individual candidates on a preferential basis
Description	Using the Droop formula, a quota is worked out. Once a candidate reaches the quota they are elected. The candidate with the fewest votes is eliminated and votes reallocated preferentially until the quota is reached and so on until all seats are filled
Where used	Northern Irish Parliament and Scottish local council

STV is the most proportional electoral system used in the UK. It is used in Northern Ireland as a means of ensuring widespread party representation as part of the Good Friday Agreement in 1998.

Table 21 Advantages and disadvantages of STV

Advantages of STV	Disadvantages of STV
■ Outcomes are proportional. ■ STV helps to ensure votes have equal value. ■ The final result is likely to be a government backed by 50% of the electorate. ■ Voters have a wide degree of choice across parties and candidates. ■ There will be very few wasted votes.	■ The MP–constituency link is lost. ■ It is complicated, leading to many spoiled ballots. ■ It is likely to produce multi-party governments which may be unstable or have a weak mandate. ■ It can lead to ill-informed donkey voting. ■ The whole process means it takes a long time to get a result. ■ People's fifth or sixth choice vote is not really considered a worthwhile vote.

Key term

Donkey voting Where voters just rank candidates in order without thinking.

The additional member system (AMS)

Table 22 The workings of AMS

Type	Hybrid (FPTP and closed party list)
Constituency size	Small, single member and large regional constituencies
Number of votes per person	Two, one for a candidate under FPTP and one for a party under closed party list
Voting for	A single candidate and a party
Description	The candidate votes are counted and declared. Based on the results of the party list votes, party seats are 'topped up' from a list of candidates to ensure fairer representation
Where used	Scottish Parliament, Welsh Assembly, Greater London Assembly

Table 23 Advantages and disadvantages of AMS

Advantages of AMS	Disadvantages of AMS
■ It retains the best bits of FPTP. ■ It allows for a more proportional representation. ■ Voters have greater choice and can split their votes. ■ The party list element allows some parties to increase the number of BAME and women candidates. ■ It has eliminated the winner's bonus in the devolved areas. ■ With enough support, single-party government is possible. ■ It allows voters to split their vote.	■ It creates two categories of representatives who are held to account differently. ■ With low levels of additional members, the proportionality is diminished. ■ Most voters will vote the same way. ■ Parties have control over who comes where on a party list. ■ It has made it very difficult for a strong and effective government to be formed. ■ Usually a single party dominates the process.

Table 24 Comparison of electoral systems

Function	FPTP	SV	STV	AMS
Strong stable government	Yes	Yes	No	Rarely
MP–constituency link	Yes	Yes	No	Mostly
Fairness of votes to seats	No	No	Yes	Mostly
Degree of choice	Limited	Moderate	Strong	Moderate
Party control	Limited	Limited	Limited	Moderate
Keeping out extremists	Yes	Yes	No	No
Easy for voters	Yes	Moderately	No	Moderately
Speed for result	Fast	Moderately	Slow	Moderately

Table 25 Have the alternative voting systems proven to be effective?

Yes	No
Fairer results	Results not always proportional
Develop minor parties	Failures of coalition in Northern Ireland
Fewer wasted votes	Extremist parties gain representation
Coalitions have worked	Weaken MP–constituency link
Engage the electorate	More spoiled ballots
May increase turnout	Turnout low in alternative UK elections

Key term

BAME An acronym for black and minority ethnic, which covers all people of non-white or non-Anglo-Saxon/Celtic descent.

Exam tips

■ You will only be credited for talking about these electoral systems; do not be tempted to discuss any others in your exams.

■ As this is a British politics course, make sure the majority of your examples come from the use of alternative systems in the UK.

■ When considering arguments about electoral reform, it is best to consider the aims of electoral systems and contrast the merits of the different systems, as shown in Table 24.

Synoptic links

Party positions on electoral reform tend to be centred on how they do under FPTP; Conservatives and Labour tend to support it, other parties tend to demand reform.

Any reform to the voting system in the UK is also an example of constitutional reform and would also impact on the nature of Parliament and prime ministerial power.

Do you know?

1 How do elections promote democracy?

2 How does FPTP work?

3 How do SV, STV and AMS work?

4 What are the advantages and disadvantages of each system?

5 How is a system chosen for Westminster?

1.8 Referendums

You need to know

- what a referendum is
- why referendums have been held
- the impact of referendums on UK political life
- the arguments for and against using referendums in a representative democracy

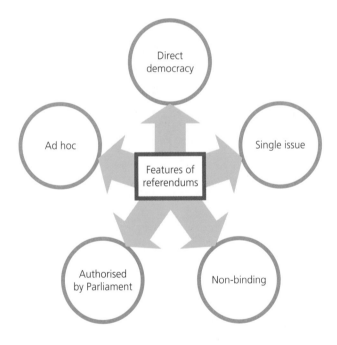

Synoptic link

As part of parliamentary sovereignty, permission to hold a referendum can only be granted by Westminster and Westminster can ignore the decision. This was confirmed by the Miller case in 2017.

National referendums

- Only three have been held.
- All three occurred when the government was weakened by a slim majority or in a coalition.

- They dealt with constitutional issues.
- Turnout reflected the importance voters attach to the issue.
- The government 'lost' the 2011 and 2016 referendums.
- All have been acted upon.

Regional referendums

- All have dealt with the transfer of power from Westminster.
- With two exceptions, turnouts have been lower than in the preceding general election.
- No result was achieved with the support of a majority of the total eligible population.
- All were authorised by Parliament.
- All were acted upon by the Westminster government and accepted by all major parties.
- Apart from Scottish Independence all were called by the government.
- Government plans were changed as a result of the 2004 North East Assembly result.

Local referendums

Key points:
- Central government has introduced metro mayors in 12 additional cities despite the referendum results.
- Most local referendums deal with policies rather than constitutional issues.
- The public accepts all council decisions on housing.
- Voters have rejected measures to increase taxation/costs.
- Turnouts have been very low.

Synoptic link

Parliament gave the authority to local councils to hold referendums in the Local Government Act, 1972 and the Localism Act, 2011.

Why have referendums been called?

Referendums have been called over:
- constitutional change: Scotland, 1997: Wales 1997: Wales 2011
- Cabinet divisions: EEC, 1975
- party divisions: EU 2016
- Coalition Agreement: AV, 2011
- testing public opinion: North East Assembly, 2004: Wales, 2011
- establishing peace: the Good Friday Agreement, 1998
- political pressure: Scotland, 2014: EU, 2016

- passing controversial decisions to voters: congestion charges and council tax increases

The Electoral Commission:
- comes up with the wording of the question
- chooses the official campaigns for each side
- regulates the involvement of any other groups
- establishes and oversees spending limits
- regulates the conduct of the campaign

Key term

The Electoral Commission Oversees the running and organisation of referendums and elections.

Referendums in a representative democracy

Table 26 Advantages and disadvantages of referendums in a representative democracy

Advantages	Disadvantages
They allow voters a direct say.	They over-simplify complex issues.
They prevent the government pursuing unpopular policies.	They undermine Parliament.
They give greater legitimacy to constitutional reforms.	They allow politicians to pass difficult decisions to the public, promoting populist politics.
They enable more participation in politics.	They can be exploited by the government to its own advantage.
They achieve some exceptionally high levels of participation.	They allow emotional, ill-informed decisions to be made.
They provide political education on core issues.	They can create public apathy.
They give some voters choices which were not offered by the parties running in their area.	They allow unaccountable groups to manipulate the public.

Do you know?

1 What is a referendum?
2 Why have referendums been called in the UK?
3 What is the role of the Electoral Commission in a referendum?
4 How do referendums improve representative democracy?
5 How do referendums undermine representative democracy?

Synoptic link

Referendums tend to promote pressure group activity as well as party activity, particularly as parties are often divided during a referendum.

1.9 Voting behaviour

You need to know

- how people choose to vote
- what class dealignment is
- what partisan dealignment is
- how class affects voting
- how gender affects voting
- how age affects voting
- how race affects voting

Individual voting choices

People vote based on individual concerns, including:

- party policies
- major issues (nationally or personally)
- how the incumbent government has done in office
- the quality of the party leader
- the image of the party, local candidate and the party as a whole
- tactical voting

In collating these concerns, voters will usually make a decision based on one of three theories:

- rational choice
- issue voting
- valence issues

There is a fourth factor, suggesting partisan voting, which is when people vote based on loyal support for a particular party, regardless of policies.

Class voting

Until the 1970s, social class most often determined voting behaviour:

- AB class (wealthy, professional highly educated) generally aligned with the Conservatives.
- DE (semi and unskilled workers, the unemployed) generally aligned with Labour.
- This meant the C1 (clerical workers) and C2 (skilled manual workers) categories would determine the result of elections and major parties focused on them.

Key terms

Tactical voting The process of using a vote to block a particular party because your preferred party is unlikely to win a seat.

Valence People vote based on the performance of the government in power.

Social class The economic group a person belongs to based on how they earn money.

Since the 1970s there has been **class dealignment** and **partisan dealignment** as voters decide how to vote based on factors other than class and their economic position.

Key points:

- The AB class and DE class have remained clearly aligned with a core party.
- Apart from 1997, C1 is typically Conservative.
- C2 have become more Conservative since 1997.
- Apart from 2017, the percentage of votes for the two main parties was declining as people voted for other parties, showing partisan dealignment.
- In 2017, the gap between the Conservatives and Labour was small in all classes, suggesting class has become a much less important factor in voting.

Table 27 Who won which class across elections, 1979–2017

Class	1979 (%)	1992 (%)	1997 (%)	2010 (%)	2015 (%)	2017 (%)
AB	Con (59)	Con (56)	Con (41)	Con (39)	Con (45)	Con (47)
C1	Con (59)	Con (52)	Lab (39)	Con (39)	Con (41)	Con (44)
C2	Lab (49)	Lab (41)	Lab (50)	Con (37)	Tie (32/32)	Con (45)
DE	Lab (57)	Lab (50)	Lab (59)	Lab (40)	Lab (41)	Lab (47)

Gender voting

Gender voting suggests that there are clear differences between how men and women cast their votes. Parties try to appeal to a particular gender by having policies that will appeal to them.

Generally, men and women consider the same things important, such as taxation, and cast their vote in much the same way.

Areas where there are differences between men and women include war, nuclear power and weapons, and differences in core priorities, with men prioritising issues such as foreign affairs and military strength, while women tend to prioritise health and education policies.

Key points:

- Before 1997, women were much more likely to vote Conservative.
- Since 1997, a higher proportion of women vote Labour.
- Men have tended to vote Conservative across the period.
- The difference in Labour/Conservative support within genders has become much narrower since 1997, suggesting gender makes much less difference to how people vote today.
- Women appear more willing to vote for other parties than men.

Exam tip

Statistics can be used in many ways to prove and disprove arguments. You will be assessed on how well you use and challenge the information in your arguments.

Table 28 Which party won the vote by gender across elections

Gender	1979	1992	1997	2010	2015	2017
Female	Con (47:35)	Con (44:34)	Lab (42:37)	Lab (31:28)	Lab (33:30)	Lab (42:40)
Male	Con (43:40)	Con (41:37)	Lab (45:31)	Con (38:36)	Con (38:37)	Con (44:43)

Age voting

Age voting suggests that parties will target voters of a particular age bracket. Parties will create economic and social policy to match the demands of particular age groups.

Key points:

- Before 1997, there was minimal party divide among the young.
- Since 1997, younger voters (below 35) tend to favour Labour far more.
- The older vote (55+) has nearly always gone Conservative, but the level of support has been increasing.
- In 1997, New Labour appealed to all age groups (or Conservatives were rejected by all).
- In 1997, support for the Conservatives increased as age increased.
- Turnout among the young tends to be much lower than among older voters, which is why Labour has been less successful in elections than the Conservatives since 1997.

Synoptic link

Election strategies will be determined by targeting key groups.

Exam tip

Make sure you know at least three examples of policies targeted at key age groups.

Table 29 Age voting across elections (Conservative vs Labour)

Age	1979	1992	1997	2010	2015	2017
18–24	Con (42:41)	Lab (38:35)	Lab (49:27)	Lab (31:30)	Lab (43:27)	Lab (62:27)
25–34	Con (43:38)	Con (40:37)	Lab (49:28)	Con (35:30)	Lab (36:33)	Lab (56:27)
35–44	Con (46:35)	Con (40:36)	Lab (48:28)	Con (34:31)	Tie (35:35)	Lab (49:33)
45–54	Con (46:35)	Con (47:31)	Lab (41:31)	Con (34:28)	Con (36:33)	Con (43:40)
55–64	Con (47:38)	Con (44:35)	Lab (39:36)	Con (38:28)	Con (37:31)	Con (51:34)
65+	Con (47:38)	Con (48:34)	Lab (41:36)	Con (44:31)	Con (47:23)	Con (61:25)

Race voting

Race voting is tightly linked to class voting, but remains important in UK elections.

Traditionally BAME voters:

■ worked in industrial jobs in cities, putting them in the C2 class
■ lived in urban areas, which tended to support Labour
■ opposed anti-immigration speeches made by prominent Conservatives

Despite changes in the class and economic background of many BAME voters, they have generally remained loyal to the Labour party while its traditional white C2 supporters have dwindled.

Key points:

■ Before 1997 race was not considered relevant in UK politics.
■ Evidence from election results pre-1997 suggests a clear majority of BAME voters voted Labour.
■ In 1997 the difference in support for Conservatives and Labour was much closer among white voters than BAME voters.
■ Since 1997, white voters have tended to support the Conservatives over Labour by 6–11%.
■ Since 1997, a large gap in party support has remained among BAME voters, closing slightly before opening again in 2017.
■ Turnout among BAME voters is typically lower (10–15%) than white voters.
■ Within BAME voters there are differences, with black voters being much more pro-Labour than Asian voters.

Table 30 Who wins based on race?

Race	1979	1992	1997	2010	2015	2017
White	n/a	n/a	Lab (43:32)	Con (38:28)	Con (39:28)	Con (35:29)
All BAME	n/a	n/a	Lab (70:18)	Lab (60:16)	Lab (65:23)	Lab (73:19)

Do you know?

1 What are the theories that explain individual voting behaviour?
2 What is the role of class, gender, age and race in elections?
3 How have voting patterns changed across at least three elections (one pre-1997, 1997 and one post-1997).
4 How is information about voting patterns used to explain the impact of these changes in elections.
5 How have changes in voting behaviour determined the outcome of elections?

1.10 Factors affecting elections

You need to know
- the role policies play in election campaigns
- how important the role of the party leader is
- what opinion polls are and how they are used
- the impact of the media in elections

Party policies

Party policies can be used to appeal to voters' self-interest, enthuse key groups of voters, inspire the party membership or to gain publicity. A good policy will help a party gain votes but a bad policy can cost it an election.

Synoptic link

Party policies are increasingly pragmatic to win elections, rather than ideological.

Table 31 Key policies in elections

Election	Policy	Impact
1979	Conservative: right to buy council houses	This motivated a number of council house residents in the C2 class to vote Conservative.
1997	Labour promised: ■ to cut class sizes ■ to punish young offenders ■ to cut NHS waiting lists ■ to cut VAT on heating ■ to reduce youth unemployment ■ not to raise taxes	These policies emphasised the third way policies and appealed to C1 and AB voters.
2017	Conservative commitment to a hard Brexit.	This won over many former UKIP voters.
2017	Labour pledged to end tuition fees.	This pledge inspired a large number of young voters to vote and to vote Labour.

Role of party leader

- Inspire party activists
- Inspire ordinary voters
- Appear prime ministerial
- Have a positive media image
- Give an appearance of strength

Synoptic link

Parties will often elect leaders with a view to winning elections, rather than for policy ideals.

Leaders in elections

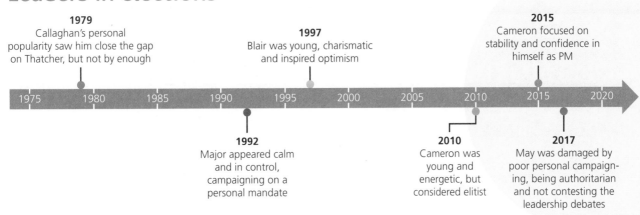

Figure 2 Leaders in elections, 1979–2017

Opinion polls

Opinion polls are used by politicians to help plan policies and campaign strategy.

Polling organisations are hired by the media and parties to find out what voters think about party policies and how they plan to vote. The results help shape news debates and help parties target key seats.

In 2015 the polls got it wrong because:

- The sample had a disproportionate number of Labour voters.
- 2015 saw a huge rise in minor party support.
- They underestimated how many Labour supporters would vote UKIP.

The mistaken polling may have influenced how people voted.

Key term

Opinion poll A sample survey that indicates support for parties or opinions.

Synoptic link

Parties use opinion polls to develop policy initiatives and manifesto ideas.

Role of the media

- Report on events
- Provide opinion on policies
- Scrutinise the government
- Investigate and raise awareness
- Educate the public
- Provide debate and discussion

Key term

Media Organisations that provide information to the public to inform, educate and entertain, covering newspapers, magazines, television, radio and the internet.

Impact of the media on elections

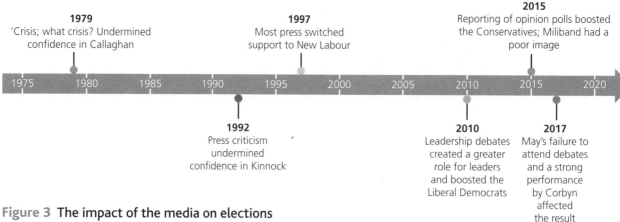

Figure 3 The impact of the media on elections

Do you know?

1 How have policies affected elections?
2 How important is the role of party leader?
3 How have opinion polls affected election campaigns and outcomes?
4 What role do the media play in scrutinising politicians?
5 How have the media shaped the political debates in the UK?

Synoptic link

In the UK political broadcasts are tightly regulated, but in the USA they are not.

Exam tip

Make sure you understand the role of the media, opinion polls and the party leader across three elections; one pre-1997, 1997 and one post-1997.

End of section 1 questions

1 What are the differences between direct and representative democracy?
2 How do elections promote democracy?
3 Is group politics beneficial to UK democracy?
4 How do rights in the UK uphold democratic principles?
5 What are the key differences in policies between the major parties?
6 What are the main divisions within the political parties?
7 How are different parties affected by FPTP?
8 Are party leaders more important than party policy?
9 Does party politics help or hinder UK democracy?
10 Is the use of referendums beneficial to representative democracy?
11 Are opinion polls too important in modern politics?
12 Does the media help or hinder the UK's system of democracy?
13 Why was 1997 a watershed election?
14 Is the Electoral Commission effective at regulating elections?
15 How democratic is the UK?

2 UK government

2.1 Development of the UK constitution

You need to know

- what a constitution is
- the differences between a codified and uncodified constitution
- how the UK constitution has evolved
- the features and functions of the UK constitution
- the different sources of the UK constitution

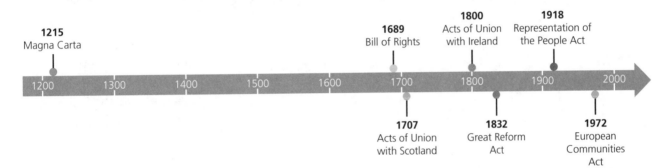

1215 Magna Carta

1689 Bill of Rights

1800 Acts of Union with Ireland

1918 Representation of the People Act

1707 Acts of Union with Scotland

1832 Great Reform Act

1972 European Communities Act

Figure 4 Development of the UK constitution

Functions of a constitution

In a liberal democracy, a **constitution** should:
- establish how a state/society is governed
- define the relationship between the state and the people
- show which bodies have which powers
- determine the relationship between different branches of government
- set out how different branches of government will work
- limit the power of government
- provide a defence for citizens from the government, through rights
- act as a higher form of law

Key term

Constitution A set of laws that determine the relationship, powers and responsibilities of the branches of government and people.

Features of the UK constitution

Table 32 Features of the UK constitution

Uncodified	It is not in one single, authoritative document. It is derived from many sources.
Unentrenched	The constitution is flexible and easy to change. Constitutional laws have the same status as ordinary laws.
Unitary	Ultimate power is centralised in one place with laws applying equally to everyone. Sovereignty is located in Parliament.
Unjudiciable	As Parliament is sovereign and there are no higher laws, judges have little power over the constitution. There are few safeguards against parliamentary abuse.

The UK constitution rests on two key principles; that Parliament is sovereign and the rule of law. This means Parliament has ultimate power and that the UK is governed by laws and legal processes.

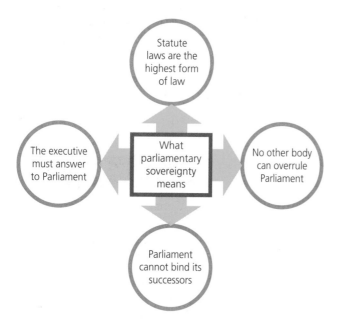

Sources of the UK constitution

The UK constitution is made up of many different sources. Sometimes these conflict with each other and sometimes rules are forgotten or unclear.

Table 33 Sources of the UK constitution

Statute laws	Laws passed by Parliament.
	They overrule any other laws.
Conventions	Unwritten customs that acquire legal status.
	These can be altered by changing practices.
Common law	Legal principles developed and applied by judges.
	Judicial review is used to establish the meaning of other laws.
Authoritative works	Works that explain the meaning and workings of the constitution.
	They are taken as legal precedents when interpreting the constitution.
Treaties	Agreements with foreign nations that impact on the workings of the UK.
	Treaties are negotiated by the government but subject to parliamentary approval.

Changing the constitution is as simple as adding a new source or altering one of the existing sources.

Do you know?

1 How has the UK constitution developed?
2 What are the key principles of the UK constitution?
3 Why is Parliament sovereign?
4 What are the key features of the UK constitution?
5 What are the main purposes of the UK constitution?
6 What are the sources of the UK constitution, and how can they be altered?

Key terms

Statute law A law passed by Parliament; an Act of Parliament.

Convention A constitutional practice that is not written down.

Common law The process of judicial rulings which create legal precedents.

Authoritative works Works that explain how the constitution operates in practice.

Treaties International agreements that impact on the way in which a country operates.

Manifesto An aggregate of policy proposals a party issues before an election.

Constitutional reform Any change to workings of the UK constitution.

Exam tip

Make sure you know how each source of the constitution can be altered, with at least one example of each.

Synoptic links

The constitutional power of Parliament often causes conflict over rights with the judiciary and the role of the executive.

The Miller case, 2017, confirmed that Parliament, not the prime minister, is responsible for triggering Article 50, and that referendums are only advisory.

2.2 Constitutional reform

You need to know

- the major constitutional reforms from 1997 to the present
- the three distinct periods of constitutional reform
- why reforms were introduced
- the impact of reforms on UK politics

When New Labour came to power in 1997, its **manifesto** was committed to a programme of **constitutional reform**. After 2001, the number for reforms slowed, but significant reforms to the workings of the UK political system still occurred up to 2010, then under the coalition 2010–15 and from the Conservative control of 2015 onwards.

1997–2010

Table 34 Constitutional reforms, 1997–2010

Reform	Detail	Impact
Lords reform	Removed all but 92 hereditary peers	■ Reduced the size of the Lords ■ Made the Lords more willing to challenge the Commons ■ Ensured no party had majority control in the Lords
Electoral reforms	New voting systems were introduced into newly created bodies and to the EU Jenkins Commission established	■ Introduced alternative voting methods to the UK ■ Showed these systems could work in the UK ■ Did cause some confusion where used ■ Nothing introduced for Westminster elections
Devolution	Some powers devolved from Westminster to bodies in: ■ Scotland ■ Northern Ireland ■ Wales ■ London Rejected in the northeast	■ Led to increasing independence of Scotland and the rise of the SNP ■ Limited impact in Wales ■ Helped to promote peace and stability in Northern Ireland, but not always successful ■ Limited impact on London ■ Rejection in the northeast ended attempts to bring devolution to English regions ■ Created the West Lothian question
The Human Rights Act	Codified the ECHR into statute law Replaced much of common law Turned negative rights into positive rights	■ Made it easier for people to defend their rights in the UK ■ Increased the power of the judiciary ■ Restricted Parliament's ability to pass laws ■ Led to conflict between Parliament and the judiciary
The Supreme Court	The Constitutional Reform Act, 2005 Created an independent Supreme Court Weakened the executive's power over appointments	■ The judiciary became physically and legally independent ■ It increased the political neutrality of judges

Synoptic links

You will need to know about the 1997 election, so knowing New Labour's policies towards constitutional reform will help your understanding of the election

Constitutional reforms are often democratic reforms, so tie in with Paper 1.

Exam tip

Make sure you are clear about which reforms occurred in which time period and how they relate to each other.

2010–15

Though less far reaching than the New Labour reforms, the Coalition's reforms had a major impact on the workings and effectiveness of Parliament.

Table 35 Constitutional reforms under the coalition

Reform	Detail	Significance
The Wright Reforms	Introduced elected chairpersons for select committees, with an additional allowance	Select committees have become more vocal and effective at scrutinising the government An alternative career path to the Cabinet
Fixed-term Parliament Act, 2011	Removed the prime minister's power to call an early election without the consent of Parliament	Power over calling early election has moved from the prime minister to Parliament Prime minister cannot make issues 'confidence motion'
Recall of MPs	Allows constituents to recall MPs who have broken the law or not attended Parliament	More power to the Speaker who decides if an MP can be recalled
Further devolution	Scotland Act 2012	Increased variable taxation for Scotland
	Wales Act 2014	Transferred some financial powers to the Welsh Assembly
Lords reform	Proposal for a fully elected House of Lords	Defeated in the House of Commons
	House of Lords Reform Act 2014	Allowed peers to retire or be removed for criminal activity or non-attendance
Electoral reform	AV referendum 2011	Referendum on changing the Westminster voting system
	PCC commissioners	SV was introduced for PCC elections

2015 onwards

Much of the post 2015 reform agenda has been dominated by Brexit, but it is not the only constitutional reform.

Synoptic link

EVEL has altered the way in which Parliament passes legislation and enhanced the role of the Speaker of the House.

Table 36 Constitutional reforms since 2015

Reform	Detail	Significance
Leaving the EU	■ Holding the EU referendum ■ Triggering Article 50 beginning a process of withdrawing from the EU as an institution	■ Enormous impact that will continue to have major impacts on the British political system for years to come
The Scotland Act, 2016	■ An Act to pass more powers to the Scottish Parliament after the independence referendum	■ Gave Scotland greater financial independence ■ New welfare powers ■ Greater legislative powers
English votes for English laws (EVEL)	■ A new legislative stage ■ The speaker is given the power to determine if a Bill is English only	■ Limited impact so far ■ Has been used but made no difference to the outcome

Codification

Table 37 Arguments for and against codifying the UK constitution

For codification	Against codification
It would give greater authority to the judiciary.	It would give an unelected judiciary too much power.
It would limit the power of government.	It would weaken the effectiveness of Parliament.
It would clarify the working of the political system.	It could become too rigid and inflexible.
The process would educate the public.	There is little public demand for it.
It would entrench basic rights.	Rights can become outdated

Do you know?

1 In what ways has the UK constitution been reformed?

2 What are the differences between New Labour and post-2010 reforms?

3 How have constitutional reforms affected other political institutions?

4 What are the arguments for and against codification?

2.3 Devolution

You need to know

- what devolution is
- why devolution was introduced
- where and how devolution operates within the UK
- the consequences of devolution

Synoptic link

Devolution is a key element of constitutional reform and has impacted on the workings of Parliament.

Aims of devolution

Devolution refers to the transfer of political power from the central to a subnational government. When devolution was introduced in 1998 it was intended to:

- enhance democracy with greater representation
- decentralise control from London
- modernise the UK political system
- reduce nationalism in Scotland and Wales
- establish peace in Northern Ireland

Exam tip

Devolution is only about the transfer of political power, not sovereignty. Sovereignty remains in Parliament as, legally, Parliament can recall powers.

Devolved bodies

Table 38 Devolution in 2018 (powers from 1998 unless shown)

	Key powers	Devolved policy areas	Size of body and electoral system	Impact
Scotland	Income tax (2016) Primary legislation Administrative	Taxation Health Environment Education Law Elections Welfare Abortion	129 MSPs in the Scottish Parliament (AMS)	Rise of SNP Scottish independence referendum Divergent policies and programme from UK (tuition fees) West Lothian question
Wales	Tax varying powers (2014) Primary legislation (2011) Administrative	Limited tax varying Health Environment Education Tourism Elections	60 Welsh Assembly members (AMS)	Growth in devolution Growth in support for devolution Variations from England (prescriptions)
Northern Ireland	Corporation tax Primary legislation Administrative	Health services Some welfare Environment Education Law Police Election	108 Assembly members (STV)	Peace Implementation of the Good Friday Agreement Power sharing, until 2017
English mayors (17 in 2018)	Administrative	Transport Education Housing Social services Planning Environmental	London Assembly = 25 AMs (AMS) Metro mayor, one per city (SV)	Transfer of administrative responsibility Local authority

Consequences of devolution

The development of devolution has created a constitutional issue with the West Lothian question and methods to solve it, like EVEL.

Changes resulting from devolution include:
- limiting parliamentary sovereignty
- creating a quasi-federal state
- creating a Joint Ministerial Committee
- an enhanced role for the Supreme Court

Key term

West Lothian question The issue of MPs from devolved areas voting in Westminster on issues that do not affect their own constituents.

Table 39 **Has devolution been beneficial for the UK?**

Yes	No
It has improved democracy by decentralising decision making.	It leads to unequal representation and the West Lothian question.
Local regions are able to prioritise local concerns.	Policy divergence means there are different standards of provision across the UK.
Peace has been brought to Northern Ireland.	It has increased nationalism and created a threat to the Union.
A sense of Britishness remains, shown in the no vote in the Scottish Independence referendum.	The nature of devolution means there is a lack of clarity and coherence on a range of policy areas.

Do you know?

1 What is devolution?

2 Why was devolution introduced?

3 What are the various powers of different devolved bodies in the UK?

4 What is the impact of devolution on the UK political system?

2.4 Workings of Parliament

You need to know

- what Parliament is and how it is structured
- the functions of Parliament
- the powers of the two chambers
- how legislation is passed
- the role of the speaker

Key terms

EVEL English Votes for English Laws was an attempt to address the West Lothian question, passed in 2015.

Parliamentary sovereignty The principle that Parliament is the supreme law-making body.

Federal A nation with a two-tier system with power divided between central government and regional governments.

Bicameral Cameral meaning 'chamber' and 'bi' meaning two, refers to Parliament comprising two chambers.

Synoptic links

The West Lothian question relates to democracy and the nature of representation.

Devolution impacts on the power of Parliament and parliamentary sovereignty.

Parliament is an assembly that meets to make and pass laws. In the UK, parliament is **bicameral**, made up of:

- the House of Commons: the elected chamber in the UK Parliament.
- the House of Lords: the unelected chamber in the UK Parliament.

Features

Tables 40 **Features of each chamber**

Commons	Lords
■ Elected by FPTP ■ Chaired by the speaker ■ Organised by party whips ■ The primary chamber ■ Enjoys parliamentary privilege ■ Regulates its own affairs	■ Unelected ■ Chaired by the Lord speaker ■ Composed of hereditary, life and spiritual peers ■ Limited by the Parliament Acts ■ Less controlled by whips ■ Not dominated by a single party

Functions

Table 41 **Functions of Parliament**

Legislate	Debate, discuss and amend Bills Vote on Bills to become Acts of Parliament
Scrutinise	Scrutinise the work of government Have an opposition tasked with holding the government to account
Debate	Debate major issues or government actions Debates can be triggered by the public through the Backbench Business Committee
Recruit ministers	Talented MPs are promoted to the government ranks MPs learn the workings of Parliament before becoming ministers
Represent	Constituency interests Party interests The UK

Key terms

Whips MPs who work for the party leader by telling party MPs what to do and how to vote.

Parliamentary privilege MPs cannot be prosecuted or sued for anything they say in the chamber of the House of Commons.

Confidence motion A vote to determine whether the Commons still supports the government. If it loses, the government must resign.

The Salisbury Convention The Lords will not vote against a proposal from a winning manifesto.

Comparative powers of the two chambers

The House of Commons is regarded as superior to the Lords due to its special powers of:

- financial privilege
- primacy over legislation
- the power to dismiss the executive

The superiority of the Commons over the Lords is upheld by the following laws and conventions:

- the Parliament Acts of 1911 and 1949
- the Lords cannot vote against any money bills
- only the Commons may defeat the government on a **confidence motion**
- **The Salisbury Convention** prevents the Lords voting against a winning party's manifesto

- the 'reasonable time convention' prevents the Lords from delaying government business
- the Lords rarely block **secondary legislation**

Since the reform of the House of Lords in 1999, the Lords has become more effective at reviewing government legislation, checking the executive and representing public concerns. This is because:

- The reformed House of Lords has a large number of cross-benchers and no overall party in control.
- The reformed House of Lords has greater expertise on policy areas than a Commons comprised of career politicians.
- With no majority winner in 2010 and 2017, the Salisbury convention does not apply.
- Less unified parties mean Lords amendments are more likely to be supported by backbench MPs.

Passage of legislation

Any **Bill** must go through five stages in each chamber before it can progress.

Key terms

Secondary legislation Legislation relating to how Acts are carried out and interpreted.

Bills Proposed laws introduced into Parliament for consideration.

Public Bill Committees A small committee responsible for considering a Bill in detail and making amendments.

Committee of the Whole House When the whole chamber acts as a revising committee on a Bill.

Royal assent the monarchs signature on a Bill, which turns it into an Act of Parliament.

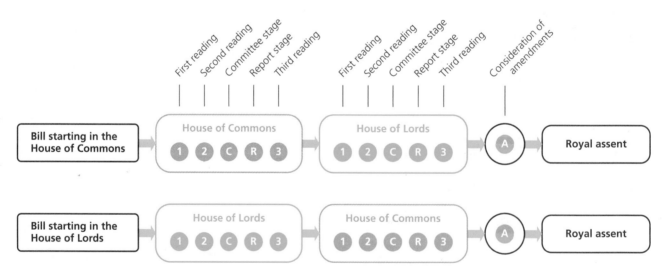

Figure 5 The British legislative process

If a Bill is passed on all five stages, it repeats the process in the other chamber. Once passed by the second chamber, both chambers consider any proposed amendments. Once a final version of the Bill has been passed, it goes to the monarch to receive Royal assent. Royal assent turns the Bill into an Act of Parliament and makes it a law of the land.

2.5 Parliament and government

MPs who do not hold a post in the government or the shadow government are called 'backbenchers'. They are the members who do the main work of Parliament, particularly in scrutiny and representation.

Select committees

There is one select committee for each government department. Their purpose is to provide specialist scrutiny of the relevant department. They typically have 11 members, reflecting party make-up in the Commons.

Select committees **can**:
- choose what issues to investigate
- call witnesses from inside and outside politics
- access restricted documents
- question witnesses
- publicise issues
- report their findings to the House of Commons

Select committees **cannot** enforce their recommendations.

Select committees are important because they:
- scrutinise government strategy, policy, spending and appointments
- scrutinise legislation and its implementation
- advise the Commons on legislation
- produce reports for the Commons to consider
- engage the public
- make politics accessible

Key terms

Backbenchers Ordinary MPs who do not sit on the government or opposition front benches.

Select committees Departmental committees that investigate and enquire into the workings of a government department.

Exam tip

Parliamentary power relates to the power of the government; things that make Parliament more powerful make the executive weaker and vice versa.

Synoptic link

There is a fusion of powers between Parliament and the executive, so the topics need to be studied in conjunction.

Table 42 **Strengths and weaknesses of select committees**

Strengths	Weaknesses
Detailed scrutiny of government policies and actions	Government majority on committees (usually)
Power to call witnesses and access government documents	Evasion of difficult questions
Authority to recommend to the government	No power of enforcement
Increasing independence since 2010	Members can use select committees to advance their own careers

Non-departmental select committees

Table 43 **Non-departmental select committees**

Liaison Committee	Made up the chairs of departmental select committees
	Questions the prime minister twice a year
Public Accounts Committee	Examines government expenditure
	Ensures the tax payer gets value for money
Public Administration and Constitutional Affairs Committee	Examines constitutional reform
	Examines the role of the civil service

Key terms

Liaison Committee A biannual meeting of the chairpersons of the select committees to quiz the prime minister.

Opposition Those MPs who do not support or form part of the government.

The opposition

The largest party not in the government forms the official opposition, which:

- forms a government in waiting
- has right of first response to the government
- scrutinises specific departments
- receives an opposition fund to help challenge the government

Limitations on the opposition

- Government usually holds a majority.
- It is often reactive rather than proactive.
- The government enjoys the assistance of the civil service.
- The official opposition is only one of the opposition parties.
- It tends to receive lower media attention.

Questions

Any MP has the opportunity to ask a question of a government minister, either on behalf of their constituents or to scrutinise the work of the minister. Questions can be oral or written.

Table 44 Parliamentary questions

Ministerial	Time is set for each department to answer questions in the Commons.
	Any MP can ask a question, on behalf of their constituents or to scrutinise the workings of the department.
Prime minister's	A weekly session for MPs to question and scrutinise the prime minister.
	Mostly seen as a contest between the prime minister and leader for the opposition.
Urgent	Require a minister to come before the House to explain an urgent matter.
	Decided by the Speaker, these have been increased under Bercow.

Synoptic link

PMQs is the most watched political event each week, so politicians 'play up to the camera' meaning the media undermines the effectiveness of Parliament.

Parliament and the government

Factors affecting the relationship between Parliament and government include:
- the size of the government's majority
- the unity of the governing party/parties
- the popularity of the PM
- the nature of issues faced
- the strength of the opposition

Parliament's power over the government decreases with:
- a larger government majority
- a unified governing party
- a popular PM
- uncontroversial issues
- a weak or divided opposition

Key reforms

After the elective dictatorship of the New Labour era, reforms were introduced to redress the balance between Parliament and the government.

The Wright Reforms

- Election of select committee chairs: made the chairs more independent from government control.
- A salary for select committee chairs: created an alternative career path to joining the government for able MPs or former ministers.

- The creation of the Backbench Business Committee: gave MPs more control over setting the agenda in Parliament.
- The introduction of e-petitions: has increased public engagement and made Parliament more democratic/answerable to the public.

The Fixed-term Parliament Act, 2011

- The prime minister cannot trigger an early election without the consent of Parliament.
- An early election request requires a 2/3 vote, more than most governing parties will have.
- The prime minister cannot simply make any issue a confidence issue, making it harder for PMs to control rebellious backbench MPs.

> **Synoptic link**
>
> Reforms to Parliament are also constitutional reforms and usually attempt to make the UK system more democratic too.

Table 45 Have the 2010 reforms made Parliament a more effective check on the government?

Yes	No
Parliament has gained some control over the parliamentary timetable.	The Backbench Business Committee only has a limited number of days outside of government control, typically 10 a year.
Select committees have become more independent and willing to scrutinise the executive.	Select committees are still dominated by government MPs. Select committees lack enforcement powers.
The prime minister must ask Parliament's permission to call an election.	On its first test Parliament supported the prime minister in 2017.
The reduction in confidence motions weakens the prime minister's power over rebellious MPs.	The whips and party loyalty mean the government is rarely defeated in the Commons.

> **Exam tip**
>
> Consider whether the 2010 reforms have made Parliament more effective at scrutinising the government or whether it has been the lack of large (or any) majorities by a single, unified party since then.

Do you know?

1 What are the factors that affect the relationship between the executive and Parliament?
2 What are select committees, and how do they work?
3 What is the role of the opposition?
4 What is the importance of parliamentary questions?

2.6 Structure of the executive

You need to know

- what the executive is
- the role of the executive in the UK
- what comprises the UK executive
- what the core executive is

The executive is the branch of government that makes things happen. It 'executes' the laws and decisions made in Parliament and runs the nation on a day-to-day basis.

Executive functions include:

- making **policy**
- making decisions
- proposing legislation
- proposing a budget

The whole government is vast, but the **core executive** consists of senior political figures and top **civil servants**.

The UK executive is made up of the following elements:

- the prime minister
- the prime minister's office
- the Cabinet
- the Cabinet Office
- junior ministers
- government departments
- the civil service

Key terms

Policy The aims and strategies of the government.

Core executive The central group of advisors and ministers who work with the prime minister.

Civil servants Those people employed by the state to carry out the day-to-day running of government institutions.

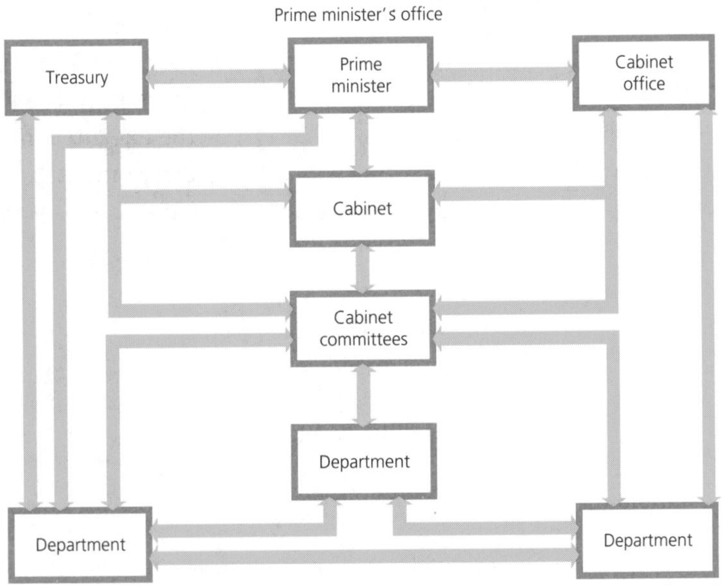

Prime minister's office

Treasury — Prime minister — Cabinet office

Cabinet

Cabinet committees

Department

Department   Department

Figure 6 The UK executive

Powers of the executive

The prime minister holds the prerogative powers of the monarch, which include the power to:

- make treaties
- meet world leaders
- command the military
- run the civil service
- issue patronage and pardons

Some prerogative powers have been reduced or removed as a result of new laws and conventions.

Table 46 Reduced prerogative powers

The power to call an early election	Ended by the Fixed-term Parliament Act, 2011
The right to declare war	Limited by convention after Blair and Iraq and Cameron and Syria
Freedom of patronage	Reduced by the creation of independent advisory committees the Joint Action Committee and the Lords Appointments Committee.

Additional powers

In addition to prerogative powers, the executive can also:

- control the legislative agenda
- make and amend delegated legislation

Delegated legislation means the executive has some legislative power in interpreting **how** laws are to be applied.

Do you know?

1 What is meant by the executive?

2 How is the UK executive structured?

3 What powers does the UK executive hold?

4 How have the executive's powers been limited?

Synoptic link

The royal prerogative is held by a convention. The changes outlined in Table 46 reflect the nature of the UK constitution; two were passed by statute law, which is superior to conventions, while the middle one was a new convention that updated an old one.

Key term

Delegated legislation Secondary legislation, where ministers make decisions on how to implement laws.

Synoptic link

The power of the executive reflects the areas that Parliament can and cannot impose its will on the executive branch of government.

2.7 The prime minister

You need to know
- how prime ministers are chosen
- the role of the prime minister
- the powers of a prime minister
- how effectively prime ministers can use their powers
- what makes a prime minister strong or weak

Forming a government

To become **prime minister** a person must:
- be an MP
- be a party leader
- have the support of a majority of MPs to pass a budget
- be invited to form a government by the monarch

> **Key term**
>
> **Prime minister** The leader of the executive branch.

Table 47 **Why people have stopped being prime minister**

Election defeat	Resigned over an issue (personal or professional)	Lost support (of party or Cabinet)
Gordon Brown	David Cameron	Tony Blair
John Major	Harold Wilson	Margaret Thatcher
James Callaghan	Harold Macmillan	

Functions of the prime minister

- **Leadership:** shaping policy and acting as the spokesperson for the government.
- **Running the government:** hiring and firing ministers, chairing Cabinet meetings and organising the civil service.
- **Exercising the prerogative powers:** managing the armed services and making public appointments.
- **Working with Parliament:** setting the agenda in the Queen's Speech and answering questions in Parliament.
- **Representing the UK:** attending international summits and conferences as well as signing treaties.

Powers of the prime minister

All prime ministers have the same powers, or tools, to achieve their aims. It is these tools that give prime ministers their power.

Table 48 Powers of the prime minister

Patronage	Appointing to government posts
	Creating supportive life peers
	Offering honours in the honours system
Control of the Cabinet system	Appointing, dismissing and promoting people to ministerial posts
	Creating government departments
	Chairing Cabinet meetings
	Setting the agenda
Policy making	Writes the Queen's Speech to set the legislative agenda
	Can push departments to follow a particular course
	Sets the overall tone for government action
Party leadership	As leader of the biggest party, prime ministers usually control a majority of MPs and therefore Parliament
	Unifying the party can create an elective dictatorship
Public image	A popular prime minister with a strong public image will have more authority over their party and Parliament
	Reputation carries a lot of weight in national and international negotiations

Limits on prime ministerial power

All prime ministers have the same core powers. However, how effectively they can exercise them depends on several factors. If factors are not favourable, a prime minister becomes weaker.

- **Size of majority:** a large majority means you can risk rebellions, but a small or no majority makes it difficult to pass laws.
- **Party unity:** if the party supports the prime minister and they have a majority, he/she can achieve anything, but if the party is divided it makes it difficult to pass laws and makes the prime minister appear weak.
- **Cabinet support:** a loyal and able Cabinet will follow the prime minister's agenda, while a Cabinet of rivals who lose faith in the prime minister can force him or her out. When it comes to Cabinet votes, the prime minister is 'first among equals'.
- **Events:** events that are uncontroversial and handled well give the prime minister authority, but contentious events or poor handling of them can undermine the prime minister's authority.

> ## Key term
>
> **First among equals** A term used to describe the prime minister's status in the Cabinet.

- **Media portrayal:** a supportive media can enhance a prime minister's reputation and support, while a hostile media can undermine confidence in the prime minister and make him or her appear weak.

Exam tip

Prime ministers usually go through phases of being strong and phases of being weak, so it is useful to think about how individual prime ministers can be seen as both.

Strong vs weak prime ministers

Table 49 Prime ministers and power

Prime minister	Strengthened by	Weakened by
Theresa May	Public Cabinet support	Lack of majority, events, media portrayal
David Cameron	Majority (after 2015), unified party	Coalition, losing Syria vote, losing referendum
Gordon Brown	Having a majority, initial media praise	The financial crisis, divided party, poor media portrayal
Tony Blair	Large majorities, initially unified party, positive media image, weak opposition	Cabinet resignations over Iraq, increasingly hostile media, divided Cabinet, Cabinet rival in Brown
John Major	Winning a majority	Losing majority, divided party, poor media portrayal, financial crash of 1992
Margaret Thatcher	Large majorities (after 1983), weak opposition, iron lady image, success in the Falklands War	Losing Cabinet support, losing party support, declining media image after poll tax riots

Are prime ministers presidential?

There is an idea that prime ministers have become more presidential in their style of leadership in recent years. This is based on the idea that:

- there is more personalised and spatial leadership
- prime ministers are given a higher media profile
- there has been an increase in leadership debates
- there has been a growth of the Downing Street machine
- there has been a rise of national 'crises'
- Cabinet has been marginalised
- there is increased use of think tanks over parties

However, this all depends on the nature of the prime minister and his/her strength in leadership.

Key terms

Presidentialism A style of leadership that focuses on behaving like a president, separate from Parliament, rather than as one among equals in the Cabinet or Parliament.

Spatial leadership The idea that there is 'space' or distance between the prime minister and the rest of government and his/her party; a more individual style of leadership.

Do you know?

1 Why have people stopped being prime minister?
2 What are the functions of the prime minister?
3 What are the powers of the prime minister?
4 What are the factors that affect the ability of the prime minister to exercise his/her powers?

2.8 The Cabinet

You need to know

■ how Cabinets are created
■ how the Cabinet is structured
■ the role of the Cabinet
■ collective and individual ministerial responsibility
■ factors that determine the power of the Cabinet
■ whether the Cabinet or prime minister is stronger

The Cabinet

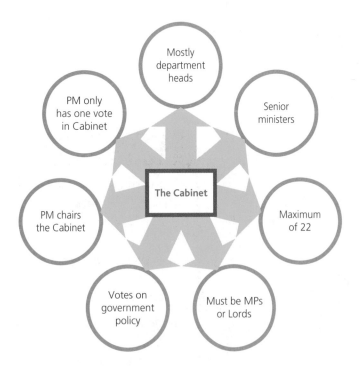

Key term

The Cabinet The government made up of the prime minister and the heads of government departments.

How Cabinets are created

Cabinet ministers are appointed by the prime minister. A prime minister must consider these factors when creating a Cabinet:

- **Party unity:** need to balance different interests from his/her party.
- **Big beasts:** prominent politicians need to be in the Cabinet.
- **Allies:** friends and allies need to be rewarded.
- **Ability:** able ministers should be promoted to Cabinet positions.
- **Experience:** either ministerial experience or departmental experience.
- **Coalition:** under a coalition, agreement on a number of Cabinet posts may be promised to the junior partner.
- **Issues:** personal scandals can lead to Cabinet removals.

Ministerial responsibility

Collective responsibility

The executive is not just the prime minister, but all senior and junior ministers as well, about 120 MPs in total.

Collective responsibility means that:

- Cabinet discussion and disagreements are kept secret.
- Decisions made by the Cabinet are binding on all ministers; anyone not accepting must resign.
- If the government is removed by a confidence vote, all ministers must resign.

The prime minister can choose to relax the rules on collective ministerial responsibility in the following circumstances:

- during referendums
- during coalitions
- during a free vote on a major issue
- to retain a key minister in the government

Individual responsibility

Ministers must be responsible and answer to Parliament for their personal conduct and the conduct of their department. They must answer questions in Parliament or in Select Committees and justify decisions and actions.

A minister must take **individual responsibility** for:

- mistakes made by their department
- failures of policy decisions and implementation
- personal misconduct (breaking the Ministerial Code of Conduct)

> ## Key terms
>
> **Collective responsibility** All ministers must publicly support the decision of the government.
>
> **Individual responsibility** Ministers are responsible for their personal conduct and the actions of their department.
>
> **The Ministerial Code of Conduct** A list of rules by which ministers are expected to abide in terms of personal and financial behaviour.

The Cabinet system

Table 50 The Cabinet system

Cabinet meetings	Usually once a week
	Fixed seating and structure
	Votes on issues where the prime minister is only one vote among all those cast and can therefore be defeated
Cabinet committees	Sub-committees appointed by prime minister for specific issues
	Smaller and more focused than full Cabinet meetings
The Cabinet Office	A civil service department that organises the Cabinet
	Cabinet secretariat carries out the key administration

Functions of the Cabinet

Table 51 Functions of Cabinet

Function	Detail
Ratifying decisions	Decisions made elsewhere (bilateral meetings, Cabinet committees etc.) should be formally ratified by the full Cabinet.
Decision making	Major issues can still be decided on by a formal discussion and vote in a full Cabinet meeting.
Settling disputes	Disputes between senior ministers or government departments can be resolved during a meeting of the full Cabinet.
Representing departments	A Cabinet minister is expected to champion the interests and needs of their department.
Advising the prime minister	Cabinet receives reports on parliamentary business, economic affairs, home and foreign issues. Based on these reports, Cabinet ministers can seek clarification and give advice to the prime minister.

Strengths and weaknesses of the Cabinet

Officially the UK has a Cabinet system and the Cabinet is the ultimate decision-making body but, with the rise of presidentialism, Cabinet has been marginalised as prime ministers use the Downing Street machine, bilateral meetings and agenda setting to ensure they can dominate the Cabinet system.

Table 52 Strengths and weaknesses of the Cabinet

Strengths	Weaknesses
Cabinet can vote to defeat the prime minister.	The prime minister sets the agenda and chooses when to hold a vote.
Department heads have expertise over specific policies.	The prime minister sets the overall policies of the government.
Cabinet is the ultimate decision-making body.	Most decisions are now made in bilateral meetings and Cabinet committees.
The prime minister usually needs to include a range of party members.	The prime minister has the ultimate power of appointment, promotion and dismissal.
Cabinet is free to discuss and debate issues.	Cabinet is bound by collective responsibility.

Synoptic link

The power of the Cabinet changes over time and is the inverse of the prime minister's powers. Cabinet will be more powerful when:
- there is little or no government majority
- the governing party is divided
- the prime minister has a weak media presence
- there are major controversial issues

Do you know?

1 What are the factors that determine Cabinet appointments?
2 What is the importance of collective and individual ministerial responsibility?
3 What are the role and powers of the Cabinet?
4 Which factors determine the power of the Cabinet?
5 Is the Cabinet or prime minister stronger?

2.9 The Supreme Court

You need to know
- what the Supreme Court is
- what powers the Supreme Court has
- why the Supreme Court was created
- how justices are appointed
- what the rule of law is
- the difference between judicial independence and neutrality

Key terms

Supreme Court The top legal authority in the UK.

Constitutional Reform Act, 2005 The law that created the Supreme Court and Judicial Appointments Commission.

The judiciary The judicial branch of the government comprising all judges in the UK.

Functions of the Supreme Court

The **Supreme Court** was created in 2009 as part of the **Constitutional Reform Act, 2005**. The aims were to:
- create a clear separation between **the judiciary** and other branches of government

- create a more open and transparent appointment process
- remove the senior judges from the House of Lords

The new Supreme Court replaced the Law Lords, who had sat in the House of Lords, as well as changing the role of the lord chancellor who had been a member of Cabinet, the House of Lords and the head of the judiciary.

The Supreme Court is an **appellate** court whose main functions include:
- acting as a final court of appeal on criminal and civil cases from England, Wales and Northern Ireland
- acting as a final court of appeal for civil cases from Scotland
- clarifying the meaning of constitutional law

Much of what the Supreme Court deals with are constitutional processes, as in the Miller case, or human rights issues, as in the Belmarsh case.

Key term

Appellate A court that only hears appeals from lower courts.

Supreme Court appointments
Who qualifies?

Nominees to the Supreme Court must be:
- holders of high judicial office for at least 2 years
- or qualified practitioners for at least 15 years

The process

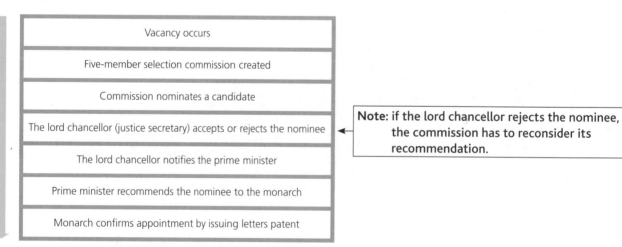

Figure 7 **How appointments are made to the Supreme Court**

Most senior judges are appointed by the **Judicial Appointments Commission (JAC)**. However, Supreme Court justices are appointed by an ad hoc five-member commission, comprising:

- the president of the Supreme Court
- the deputy president of the Supreme Court
- one member of the JAC for England and Wales
- one member of the Judicial Appointments Board for Scotland
- one member of the JAC for Northern Ireland

Key principles

The **rule of law** means:

- the right to trial by jury
- no one is above the law
- laws are applied equally
- judges protect personal freedoms

Judicial independence

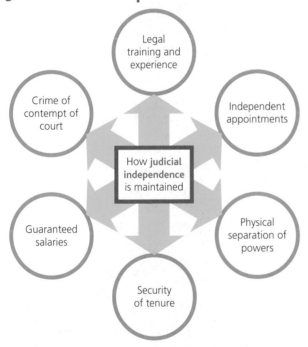

Challenges to judicial independence include:

- political controversies derived from the Human Rights Act (HRA) rulings
- the power to suspend UK laws incompatible with EU law
- the increased use of judicial review
- greater media focus and scrutiny of the judiciary in a political context
- public criticisms made by politicians

Key terms

Judicial Appointments Commission (JAC) An independent body created to recommend judicial appointments to the prime minister.

Rule of law The idea that justice is applied equally to all UK citizens.

Judicial independence The principle that judges are not controlled or influenced by other branches of the government.

Synoptic links

Democratically, some argue the Supreme Court should reflect the population of the UK, but in 2018, 10/12 had been to private school, 9/12 had attended Oxbridge, all were over 60 and only 2 are women.

The principles of the rule of law are set out by A. V. Dicey in an authoritative text.

Judicial neutrality

Challenges to judicial neutrality include:

■ limited range of backgrounds
■ increasing media profile and scrutiny
■ increasing willingness to criticise the government
■ the lack of legal precedent regarding Brexit
■ judges' own personal prejudices

Power of the Supreme Court

Judicial review

The main powers of judges are to carry out **judicial review** and clarify points of law.

Judges can:

■ declare ministerial actions to be *ultra vires*
■ declare primary laws incompatible with the HRA
■ declare and suspend laws incompatible with European law until British withdrawal from the EU

The power of judicial review has increased due to:

■ the importance of EU law in the UK
■ the codification of the European Convention on Human Rights into UK law under the Human Rights Act, 1998

Complaints can be taken to two higher courts:

- the European Court of Human Rights (not EU)
- the European Courts of Justice (dealing with EU law, such as the Factortame case)

The strength of judicial review can be contrasted in two key cases:

- The Miller case: Supreme Court decision of 2017 that determined Parliament, not the prime minister, had the right to trigger Article 50.
- The Belmarsh case: a 2004 ruling that the rights of non-EU terror suspects were being denied.

Growing importance of the Supreme Court

Why judicial importance has grown	Why judicial importance has not grown
<ul><li>It is more independent since the physical separation</li><li>The ECHR is now part of UK law</li><li>Factortame allows it to suspend some statute laws</li><li>It has the power to suspend actions of the executive under the HRA</li><li>EU law has become part of UK law</li><li>Laws are made to comply with the HRA</li><li>The impact of Brexit</li></ul>	<ul><li>Parliament can ignore declarations of incompatibility</li><li>Parliament remains sovereign</li><li>The government can control Parliament to amend laws</li><li>The judiciary remains a weak branch of government</li><li>The UK constitution is uncodified</li></ul>

The judiciary and democracy

Table 53 **Is the judiciary a positive in a democracy?**

Yes	No
It acts as a check on Parliament and the executive.	It is unelected, unlike the other branches.
It promotes human rights through judicial review.	It focuses on individual rather than social rights.
It is politically independent.	It is not accountable for decisions.
It is politically neutral.	It is not representative of the UK.
Members are experts in the law.	Members tend to come from an elite background.

Do you know?

1 Why was the Supreme Court created?
2 How are justices appointed?
3 What are the powers of the Supreme Court?
4 What is the nature of judicial independence and neutrality?
5 What are the positives and negatives of the judiciary in the UK democracy?

2.10 The EU

You need to know

- the aims of the EU
- the role and functions of the EU
- key EU institutions
- the impact of the EU on the UK
- the reasons for and impact of Brexit

Aims of the EU

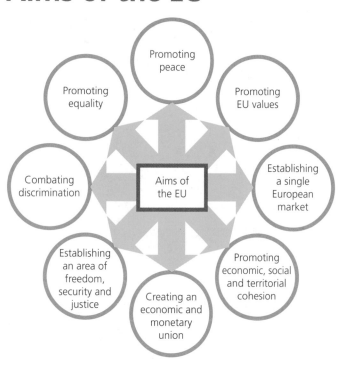

The values of the EU include:

- human dignity
- freedom
- democracy
- equality
- the rule of law
- respect for human rights

The single market is based on the four freedoms; free movement of goods, services, people and capital. Within this, the EU has the eurozone, comprised of 19 members who all share the same currency.

Synoptic link

The values of the EU relate closely to the democracy section of the course.

EU institutions

There are five key EU institutions:

- the European Commission
- the Council of the European Union
- the European Council
- the European Parliament
- the Court of Justice of the European Union

The European Commission

Commissioners are nominated by national governments and approved by the European Parliament.

The Commission:

- initiates draft legislation
- executes EU legislation
- administers EU spending
- represents the EU internationally

The Council of the European Union

The Council of the European Union is made up of ministers chosen by and representing the 28 member states. Decisions must be made either unanimously or by qualified majority voting (55% of member states representing 65% of the EU population).

The Council of the European Union:

- shares legislative powers with the European Parliament
- coordinates economic policy
- develops the EU's foreign and security policies

The European Council

The European Council is made up of the member states' heads of government or heads of states and their foreign ministers, meeting four times a year.

The European Council:

- discusses major issues
- sets the EU's political direction
- makes decisions on EU foreign and economic policy
- agrees to treaty changes
- launches new initiatives

The European Parliament

The European Parliament is made up of 751 MEPs elected every 5 years by EU citizens. Seats are allocated proportionately.

The European Parliament:
- legislates (but cannot initiate legislation)
- authorises and amends the EU budget
- gives democratic legitimacy to appointed elements
- scrutinises the work of the other branches

The Court of Justice of the European Union

Based in Luxembourg, the Court is a final court of appeal for cases relating to EU law, institutions, business and individuals.

The Court of Justice:
- clarifies EU law for member states
- makes rulings on areas of conflict or uncertainty

The EU and UK

Agreeing to be in the EU meant accepting EU law into British law. This placed restrictions on UK sovereignty by:
- accepting the primacy of EU law
- giving courts the power to suspend statute law incompatible with EU law
- banning independent trade agreements

In theory, many of these powers will return to the UK after Brexit.

The main areas of difficulty between the UK and EU concerned:
- the Common Agricultural Policy
- the Common Fisheries Policy
- the EU budget and the UK's contribution
- the Social Chapter and workers' rights
- immigration and the free movement of labour

The decision to leave the EU

In June 2016 the UK held a referendum on EU membership. A majority (52:48%) voted to leave, triggering the process of Brexit.

Reasons why people voted to leave included:
- the loss of sovereignty to the EU
- concerns over EU policies

- concerns about immigration
- popular nationalism
- popular Euroscepticism
- concerns about the cost of EU membership

Do you know?

1 What are the main aims of the EU?
2 What are the four freedoms of the single market?
3 What are the main institutions of the EU, and what powers do they have?
4 Which areas have seen conflict between the UK and EU?
5 Why did the UK voted to leave the EU?

End of section 2 questions

1 Why has the UK constitution been criticised?
2 How significant has constitutional reform been?
3 Should the UK constitution be codified?
4 How effective a check is Parliament on the government?
5 How representative is Parliament?
6 Why has the House of Lords been reformed?
7 Which chamber of Parliament is more powerful?
8 How has the role of the prime minister changed in recent years?
9 Why has the role of the media changed the role of the prime minister?
10 How powerful is the Cabinet?
11 Why was the Supreme Court created?
12 Why is the Supreme Court controversial?
13 What impact will Brexit have on the judiciary?
14 Has the EU been successful?
15 Why did the UK vote to leave the EU?

3 Ideologies

3.1 Liberalism

You need to know

- the core ideas of liberalism
- how the core ideas relate to human nature, the state, society and the economy
- the differing views and tensions within liberalism
- the key ideas of:
  - ☐ Locke
  - ☐ Wollstonecraft
  - ☐ Mill
  - ☐ Rawls
  - ☐ Friedan

Liberalism developed over the seventeenth and eighteenth centuries as a reaction against the concepts of divine rights of the king, religious obedience and set hierarchies of medieval societies. It was based on science, reason and philosophy.

Core ideas

Table 54 Core ideas of liberalism

Idea	Meaning	Related concepts
Individualism	Individuals are supreme. Individuals will apply logic and reason. A positive view of human nature. Self-interest is a prime motivator. Individuals will obey natural laws that temper their self-interest.	Individualism Egotistical individualism
Rationalism	Individuals will apply logic and reason and do what makes rational sense. Individuals will act in their own, rational, self-interest but also what is rationally in the best interests of society.	

▶

Idea	Meaning	Related concepts
Liberty	The freedom to make your own choices. Society is strongest when individuals are free to pursue their own goals without regulation or restrictions. Such freedoms exist under natural laws, which it is irrational to break.	Economic liberalism Individualism
State	Government rules with the consent of the governed, through a social contract. Mankind is capable of creating a state. The state should be limited by having a constitution and individual rights. State power and institutions should be separated. Tolerance of individualism and diversity.	State of nature Social contract Limited government Rights protection Separation of powers Mechanistic theory
Equality	Individuals are born equal. Equality exists under the rule of law. There should be equality of opportunity for everyone. Different views and behaviours are to be tolerated as individual choices.	Social justice Foundational equality Toleration Formal equality
Liberal democracy	Promotion of a limited government with rights protections. Government rules by the will of the people, through elections, referendums and so on, but the government is able to ensure society is free. Society is based on a meritocracy.	Civil rights Civil liberties Democracy

Key terms

Social contract The government rules by the consent of the people and if it breaks this agreement it can be replaced.

Limited government State institutions are restricted in power by constitutional laws and rights.

Tolerance Activities and behaviours should be accepted and permitted if they do not harm others.

Mechanistic theory Mankind is capable of creating a state to meet its needs.

Foundational equality People are born equal and therefore entitled to equal protection of the law.

Formal equality Equality of opportunity is protected through formal laws.

Equality of opportunity All people should start with the same possibility of succeeding and developing.

Meritocracy Social, economic and political advancement should be based on individual worth and ability.

Types of liberalism
Classical liberalism

Classical liberalism believes in:

- **Revolutionary potential:** if/when a government or institutions become too powerful and infringe on individual liberties, the people are entitled to rise up in revolution and overthrow the government, but private property must be respected.
- **Negative liberty:** everything is legal until it is prohibited, meaning a person is free to do as they please until it is expressly banned or restricted. The fewer restrictions, the great the liberty.

- **Minimal state:** while a state is necessary, it should do little and only when required, such as legislating and taxing.
- **Laissez-faire capitalism:** economic measures should be left to market forces without interference or restrictions from the state, such as duties, tariffs, taxes and regulations. Private property must be protected.

Key thinkers include:
- John Locke
- Mary Wollstonecraft
- John Stuart Mill

Modern liberalism

Modern liberalism believes in:
- **Positive liberty:** market forces and social conditions limit individual freedoms, so individual liberty needs to be clearly protected by introducing laws. This would allow social justice and equality to be achieved.
- **Enlarged state:** in order to protect individuals from socioeconomic threats, it is the role of the state to act through collective measures, and enlarging the role of the state through taxation, regulation and legislation.
- **Constitutional reform:** to enable the enlargement of the state, constitutional reform is necessary to ensure the state remains democratic, representative and limited, while also carrying out more functions.
- **Social liberalism:** actively promoting toleration by passing laws to punish those who are not tolerant of others.

Key thinkers include:
- John Rawls
- Betty Friedan

Comparing types of liberalism

Classical and modern liberalism disagree over:
- negative and positive freedoms
- the size and role of the state
- rates of taxation
- laissez-faire and Keynesian capitalism
- levels of democracy and respect for private property

Classical and modern liberalism agree over:
- a positive view of human nature
- the importance of individualism

- rationalism and toleration
- the principle of capitalism
- a government based on consent and limited by constitutional protections

Key thinkers

Table 55 Key thinkers and themes

Thinker	Human nature	Government	Society	Economy
John Locke	Humans are rational and self-interested, but mindful of others.	Rules by the consent of the governed.	Natural laws guide social relations, not laws.	The state should respect private property and act as a neutral arbiter.
Mary Wollstonecraft	Men and women are rational beings.	Republican with enshrined women's rights.	A patriarchal society has undermined female individualism.	Liberated women would boost a free-trade economy.
John Stuart Mill	Human nature is progressing to higher levels.	Representative democracy with respect for minority rights.	A society of individuality and self-improvement.	Laissez-faire capitalism was the route to a happy and successful society.
John Rawls	Humans are selfish and empathetic.	The state has a duty to assist the less fortunate.	The condition of the poorest should be improved.	Free-market capitalism should be restricted.
Betty Friedan	Human nature discourages self-advancement for women.	The state has a duty to prevent discrimination against women.	Society is chauvinistic with women being complicit in this.	Anti-discrimination legislation would boost the free market.

Do you know?

1 What are the core ideas and principles of liberalism?
2 How do the core ideas and principles relate to human nature, government, society and the economy?
3 What different types of liberalism exist?
4 On which areas do the different types agree and disagree?
5 Which types of liberalism are the core thinkers associated with?

3.2 Conservatism

You need to know

- the core ideas of conservatism
- how the core ideas relate to human nature, the state, society and the economy
- the differing views and tensions within conservatism
- the key ideas of:
  - ☐ Hobbes
  - ☐ Burke
  - ☐ Oakeshott
  - ☐ Rand
  - ☐ Nozick

Conservatism was an ideological reaction against liberalism. Shocked by the violence and chaos of the French Revolution, conservative thinkers promoted a return to hierarchy and order in society with limited change when needed. Deference to superiors, respect for traditional institutions and a negative view of human behaviour underpinned their thinking.

Core ideas

> **Key term**
>
> Empiricism Judgements based on experience.

Table 56 Core ideas of conservatism

Idea	Meaning	Related concepts
Pragmatism	Decisions are made based on what is needed and beneficial. An ideological agenda is not pursued but decisions are reached in reaction to organic problems that emerge.	Organic society
Tradition	Traditional customs and methods provide structure to society. Lessons should be drawn from history and experience. Change should happen slowly and in small steps.	Respect for property Nation-state **Empiricism** Christian democracy
Human imperfection	Behaviour is shaped by environment, not by individuals. Humans are inherently selfish and need to be controlled through laws and restrictions.	Original sin Judaeo-Christian morality Order and authority
Organic society	Society is more important that the individual. Society emerges over time, and evolves without being created.	Tradition
Paternalism	Society works best when it is unequal. The wisest, strongest and wealthiest should govern society and take responsibility for the lower classes.	Hierarchy *Noblesse oblige* A ruling class

▶

Idea	Meaning	Related concepts
Libertarianism	Supports free markets and individual liberty within a nation state. Individual freedoms should be respected by governments.	Laissez-faire Thatcherism Neo-liberalism

Types of conservatism

Traditional conservatism

Traditional conservatism believes in:

- **human imperfection**
- **authority** is needed to control society through a social **hierarchy**, but those in control hold *noblesse oblige*
- society and reforms should be based on experience and tradition, and limited
- society is organic and needs to **change to conserve** the best of the past
- class divisions are inevitable
- a society of little communities

Key thinkers include:

- Thomas Hobbes
- Edmund Burke

One-nation conservatism

One-nation conservatism believes in:

- a society of classes within a strong nation state
- paternalistic duty of the rich to look after the poor
- state-sponsored social reform to counteract the permissive society
- restrictions on laissez-faire capitalism
- support for Keynesian economics, welfare states and mixed economies
- pragmatic approaches

Key thinkers include:

- Michael Oakeshott

New-right conservatism

New-right conservatism believes in:

- individual freedom and **atomism**
- reduction in taxation and government spending
- laissez-faire capitalism and free markets with deregulation and privatisation

Key terms

Human imperfection Humanity is inherently flawed and perfection is impossible to attain.

Authority A higher degree of power or status over others.

Hierarchy The idea that there will be a system of social or class structures with superior and inferior members.

Noblesse oblige The paternalistic duty of those in power.

Change to conserve Limited amounts of change are necessary to prevent more radical revolutions.

Atomism Society is composed of self-interested and self-serving individuals.

- private property
- minimal government and reduction of welfare
- tougher law and order
- strong national defence
- restrictions on immigration
- traditional social values and anti-permissiveness

Key thinkers include:
- Ayn Rand
- Robert Nozick

The new right is also fragmented into:
- **Neo-liberalism:** focused on individualism and free-market economics.
- **New-conservatism:** focused on tradition and the maintenance of traditional social and cultural values through law and order.

> **Key term**
>
> **Anti-permissiveness** A rejection of the cultural reforms of the 1960s and 1970s.

Comparing types of conservatism

Traditional, one-nation and new-right conservatism disagree over:
- a sceptical or positive view of human nature
- society: one of small communities or one that is the sum of individuals
- a strong and powerful nation state or a small and minimalist state
- the extent of free-market capitalism

Traditional, one-nation and new-right conservatism agree over:
- humanity being motivated by self-interest
- government exists to provide national security and maintain law and order
- the importance of law and order
- society is fractured
- respect for private property
- the principle of free-market capitalism

Key thinkers

Table 57 **Key thinkers and themes**

Thinker	Human nature	Government	Society	Economy
Thomas Hobbes	Individuals are selfish and ruthless.	Government exists to provide security and order.	Society is created by the state.	The economy can only exist through state protection.
Edmund Burke	Humans desire, but cannot achieve, perfection.	The state is organic and aristocratic.	Society is based on small communities.	Free markets and laissez-faire.

Thinker	Human nature	Government	Society	Economy
Michael Oakeshott	Humanity should be free within structures.	Government by tradition and pragmatism.	Humanity depends on local communities.	Free markets need to be moderated.
Ayn Rand	Humans should by guided by rational self-interest and self-fulfilment.	Minimal role (law, order and security).	There is no society, only a mass of individuals.	Free markets with no state intervention.
Robert Nozick	Self-interested in self-ownership.	The state passes public works to private sectors.	Society should promote individual self-fulfilment.	The state should only be an arbiter between private companies.

Do you know?

1 What are the core principles of conservatism?
2 What are typical conservative attitudes to human nature, government, society and the economy?
3 What are the tensions within conservative ideology?
4 What are the areas where the different types agree and disagree?
5 Which types of conservatism are the core thinkers associated with?

3.3 Socialism

You need to know

■ the core ideas of socialism
■ how the core ideas relate to human nature, the state, society and the economy
■ the differing views and tensions within socialism
■ the key ideas of:
  □ Marx
  □ Webb
  □ Luxemburg
  □ Crosland
  □ Giddens

Socialism emerged over the nineteenth century as a reaction to traditional conservatism and the growing inequalities that had emerged in industrial societies as a result of capitalism. It promoted the idea of collective action and the removal of all hierarchy to promote a system that would ensure economic equality for all.

Core ideas

Table 58 Core ideas of socialism

Idea	Meaning	Related concepts
Collectivism	Human society will be strongest when there is collective action by all humanity towards a greater good. Politics, economics and social reform should benefit society, not individuals. There should be wealth redistribution to equalise society.	Common ownership Progressive taxation Progressive public spending Public services
Common humanity	Humans are naturally social. Individuals are shaped by society and capitalism has corrupted natural social tendencies.	Anti-capitalism Fraternity
Equality	Belief that people are not born equal. Focus on equality of outcome, rather than of opportunity.	Social justice
Social class	Society is divided into classes based on how money is earned and professions with higher classes benefiting at the expense of the lower.	Class consciousness
Workers' control	Those who produce should control the means of production. A strong state is necessary to achieve a socialist state, but that state should be governed by the workers.	Communism Marxism

Types of socialism

Revolutionary socialism

Revolutionary socialism believes in:
- the destruction of the capitalist system
- the overthrow of the existing world order
- the 'creation' of a socialist state
- total state control over the economy
- a socialist or communist state would be governed by a dictatorship of the proletariat
- imposition of socialism on society
- common ownership

Key terms

Common ownership The means of production are owned collectively and profits are shared.

Fraternity The relationship between people.

Capitalism Wealth is privately owned and economies are driven by market forces.

Social justice An attempt to limit inequality through wealth redistribution.

Equality of outcome Aiding disadvantaged groups to achieve the same outcomes as other groups.

Class consciousness A self-understanding of a class by its members.

Communism All wealth and society are organised and shared communally.

Marxism The political theories of Karl Marx that communism is inevitable.

Exam tip

Be careful not to confuse revolutionary with evolutionary; evolutionary means gradual change, while revolutionary means rapid change. Both types of socialism agree on change but disagree on the speed of change.

Key thinkers include:

- Karl Marx
- Rosa Luxemburg

Democratic socialism

Democratic socialism believes in:

- the replacement of the capitalist system by a socialist system
- that a socialist state can evolve from current systems without revolution
- a socialist state will be achieved by socialist parties winning electoral majorities
- nationalisation and common ownership

Key thinkers include:

- Beatrice Webb

Social democracy

Social democracy is a branch of **revisionist socialism**, that believes capitalism and socialism can be compatible, unlike fundamental socialism, which believes capitalism must be eradicated to create a socialist state.

Social democrats believe in:

- rationality
- **evolutionary socialism**
- operating within current political structures
- a mixed economy, with socialistic elements operating within a capitalist framework
- major state involvement in the economy
- nationalisation of private industry
- **Keynesian economics**
- persuading voters of the inevitable benefits of socialism through social justice

Key thinkers include:

- Anthony Crosland

> ### Key terms
>
> **Revisionist socialism**
> An approach to socialism that believes socialism is compatible with capitalism.
>
> **Evolutionary socialism**
> Socialism will gradually be achieved within existing systems.
>
> **Keynesian economics**
> Government intervention is necessary in economics.

Third way

Third way believes in:

- a greater focus on equality of opportunity rather than equality of outcome
- liberalisation of the economy to provide more money for public spending
- privatisation over nationalisation
- a greater focus on social and political equality as well as economic equality

Key thinkers include:

■ Anthony Giddens

Comparing types of socialism

Revolutionary, democratic socialism, social democrats and third-way supporters disagree over:

■ the impact of society on human nature
■ how far human nature is corrupted by capitalism
■ the strength and power of the state
■ the speed and nature of change
■ the existence or role of capitalism within a socialist state

Revolutionary, democratic socialism, social democrats and third-way supporters agree that:

■ human nature is social and malleable
■ a nation state is essential
■ change and reforms are needed to the current system
■ the state has a duty to oversee public welfare
■ the state plays a part in the economic developments

Key thinkers

Table 59 Key thinkers and themes

Thinker	Human nature	Government	Society	Economy
Karl Marx	Humans are social creatures, but this has been damaged by capitalism.	Existing governments need to be destroyed and replaced by a socialist state.	Society should be classless.	Collective ownership.
Rosa Luxemburg	Social cohesion exists within social classes.	Existing governments need to be destroyed and replaced by a workers-based society of true democracy.	Sub-cultures provide a model for future societies.	Capitalism can only be replaced by an economy based on workers' control.
Beatrice Webb	Capitalism should be replaced by an evolutionary process.	Universal suffrage was the key to creating a socialist state.	Poverty should be tackled as a priority.	Gradual replacement of capitalism by common ownership of the means of production.
Anthony Crosland	Humans naturally oppose inequality.	Existing systems can be used to create a socialist state.	The class system is complex and many do not fit into class distinctions.	A mixed economy.
Anthony Giddens	Social fairness is combined with self-fulfilment.	Government power should be decentralised.	Socialists must work with the middle classes, not oppose them.	A neo-liberal economy to provide for welfare programmes.

Do you know?

1 What are the main ideas upon which socialism rests?
2 How does socialism relate to human nature, government, society and the economy?
3 What are the different types of socialism?
4 What are the areas of agreement and disagreement within socialism?
5 Which types of socialism are the core thinkers associated with?

End of section 3 questions

1 What are the core ideas of liberalism?
2 How do the core ideas of liberalism relate to human nature, society, the state and the economy?
3 Why is there tension between the different strands of liberalism?
4 What are the common traits of liberalism?
5 How do different thinkers relate to different strands of liberalism?
6 What are the core ideas of conservatism?
7 How do the core ideas of conservatism relate to human nature, society, the state and the economy?
8 Why is there tension between the different strands of conservatism?
9 How do different thinkers relate to different strands of conservatism?
10 What are the common traits of conservatism?
11 What are the core ideas of socialism?
12 How do the core ideas of socialism relate to human nature, society, the state and the economy?
13 Why is there tension between the different strands of socialism?
14 How do different thinkers relate to different strands of socialism?
15 What are the common traits of socialism?

4 US politics

4.1 The US Constitution

Features of the US Constitution

The US **Constitution** has three key features:
- it is **codified**, meaning in one single, authoritative document
- it is **entrenched**, meaning it is difficult to amend and judiciable
- it has many vague elements, opening it up to interpretation

As a result of these features, the US Constitution is a higher form of law than other laws, giving the USA a two-tier legal system.

The constitutional framework

The US Constitution comprises seven articles detailing the powers of different branches and the relationship between the branches and the nature of the Constitution itself.

Table 60 **The constitutional framework**

Article	Aspect	Powers
I	Legislature	All legislative powers will be held by a bicameral Congress.
II	Executive	All executive powers will be held by a single president for a 4-year term.
III	Judicial	Judicial power will be vested in a Supreme Court of the United States.
IV	Federalism	Reserved powers are held by the states, implied powers are held by the federal government, concurrent powers are shared.
V	Amendment process	Amendments can be proposed by Congress or the states and must be ratified by the people or by state legislatures.
VI	Miscellaneous provisions	Supremacy clause set the Constitution as the highest form of law in the USA.
VII	Ratification process	Gives the power to the people, through conventions, to accept the Constitution.

Key terms

Constitution A set of formal laws to govern a country.

Codified When laws are gathered into one single document.

Entrenched When laws are entrenched, they are difficult to overturn and amend.

Synoptic link

As constitutional law is higher, the US Supreme Court can strike down statute laws, unlike the UK Supreme Court, where all laws are equal.

Exam tips

- By allowing the people to ratify the Constitution, the USA became the first country to enable the people to decide how they would be ruled, making it highly democratic.
- The articles were written in the order of their importance to the Founding Fathers.

Amendments

The US Constitution has been amended (changed) 27 times since it was written.

Any amendment must go through two stages: proposal and ratification.

Table 61 The amendment process

Proposed by...	Two-thirds of the House AND the Senate OR
	Legislatures in two-thirds of the states calling for a National Constitutional Convention
Ratified by...	Three-quarters of state legislatures (38) OR
	Ratifying conventions in three-quarters of the states

Synoptic link

The debates over powers and the relationship between the branches and the federal government and the states depend on interpretations of the Constitution.

Table 62 Advantages and disadvantages of the amendment process

Advantages	Disadvantages
Any amendment will have the support of a clear majority of the USA.	5% of the population can effectively stop an amendment.
Pointless or needless amendments are not passed.	Desirable or necessary amendments cannot be made.
It preserves the sanctity of the US Constitution.	It allows the Constitution to become outdated.
Ratification retains federalism.	Complexities give too much power to the Supreme Court.

Synoptic link

This is the formal process of amending the Constitution, but the Supreme Court amends it whenever it applies judicial review, meaning the Constitution is effectively amended several times a year.

The Bill of Rights

The first ten amendments are known as 'the Bill of Rights'. This aims to protect citizens and states from the federal government.

Table 63 The Bill of Rights

Amendment	Rights
I	Freedom of religion, speech, petition, press and assembly
II	Right to bear arms
III	No quartering of troops in private homes
IV	Unreasonable stop and searches
V	Rights of the accused
VI	Right to trial by jury
VII	Common law
VIII	Cruel and unusual punishments
IX	Protection of unenumerated rights
X	Powers reserved to the states (federalism)

Exam tips

■ On any question relating to the amendment process, do not forget to include the role of the Supreme Court.
■ Some questions may ask about constitutional rights while others may ask about the Bill of Rights. Make sure you are clear on the rights specifically stated in the Bill of Rights.

Principles of the US Constitution

Aims of the **Founding Fathers**:

- democracy
- limited government
- federalism
- national government

The key **principles** of the US Constitution are:

- **separation of powers**
- **checks and balances**
- **bipartisanship**
- limited government
- federalism

Separation of powers

The different branches of the federal government are separated. They physically occupy different locations and people cannot be in two branches at once.

Different branches have different powers, but powers are in fact shared, while it is institutions that are separate.

Table 64 Separated powers

President	Congress	Supreme Court
Power to enforce laws	Power to make and pass laws	Power to review laws
Power to nominate	Power of confirmation	Power to determine constitutionality
Power to spend	Power to tax	Power to determine constitutionality

Checks and balances

The separation of powers means power is distributed between the branches so that no single branch can become too powerful or tyrannical. To limit the power of each branch, the other branches act as a check on the other two to prevent any form of dictatorship.

Table 65 Checks in the US Constitution

Checks by/on	The president	Congress	The Supreme Court
The president	X	Veto a bill	Pardon
Congress	Overriding a veto Confirmation of appointments and treaties Impeachment	X	Proposing constitutional amendments Impeachment
The Supreme Court	Declaring actions unconstitutional	Striking down unconstitutional laws	X

Bipartisanship

The Founding Fathers believed a separation of powers would force factions to compromise to create better legislation, but today **divided government** can occur between the executive and legislative branches.

While the Constitution can promote bipartisanship and compromise, it can also lead to less effective government, as partisan groups use the checks and balances to block their rivals.

Table 66 **Recent periods of divided and unified government**

Years	Presidency	House	Senate
2016+	Republican	Republican	Republican
2014–16	Democrat	Republican	Republican
2010–14	Democrat	Republican	Democrat
2008–10	Democrat	Democrat	Democrat
2006–08	Republican	Democrat	Democrat
2002–06	Republican	Republican	Republican
2001–02	Republican	Republican	Democrat

Limited government

The separation of powers, and checks and balances were designed to limit the power of the national or 'federal' government.

The Bill of Rights was introduced to ensure the power of the government was limited.

Federalism

While a strong national government was seen as necessary in 1788, the states wanted to retain their own powers and customs. The Constitution created a federal system, with a strong, but limited, national (or federal) government which would have **enumerated powers** over some areas, with state governments holding power and authority over all other areas.

However, as America changed, so did the nature of federalism, with **implied powers** being used to give more power to the federal government at the expense of the states.

Federalism since 1968

Federalism increased because:

- New federalism attempted to give more control to the states with block grants.

- Reagan attempted to reduce the size of the federal government.
- Supreme Court rulings, like *US* vs *Lopez*, began to limit the power of the federal government.

However, under Bush and Obama federalism decreased in key areas:

- **education:** No Child Left Behind and Rise to the Top
- **healthcare:** Medicare expansion and the Affordable Care Act
- **defence:** Homeland Security and increasing terror threats
- **economic:** bailouts and growing federal employment
- **environment:** the growth of the Environmental Protection Agency (EPA) and environmental initiatives

Synoptic link

Through devolution the UK appears to have federalism, but the rights of devolved bodies are granted by Parliament and not protected by the Constitution, so their power is much weaker than in the USA.

Federalism in the Constitution

Evidence of states rights and powers in the Constitution include:

- Representation and taxation was determined by state.
- State governors fill vacancies.
- All states get equal representation in the Senate.
- Representatives must reside in their state.
- Electoral processes are to be determined by the states.
- The Electoral College is based on state representation.
- Each state must respect the laws and customs of the others.
- Ratification was to be determined by the state.
- Ratification of amendments is determined by states.
- The 10th Amendment.

Democracy and the US Constitution

Many Founding Fathers had a fear of populism so introduced constitutional measures to limit democracy.

Exam tip

When considering democratic elements, it is important to consider what you mean by democracy and what the different types of democracy are.

Table 67 **Democracy in the US Constitution**

Democratic	Anti-democratic
Popular elections to the House	Senators to be appointed by state legislatures
Public involvement in amendments	The need for supermajorities can create a tyranny of the minority
An elected president	The Electoral College
Proportional representation of states	Unequal representation in the House
All states get equal representation in the Senate	Large population states are under-represented in the Senate and Electoral College
Bill of Rights protects citizens	3/5 clause and support for slave trade

UK/US comparison

Table 68 The US Constitution and UK constitution compared

US	UK
Codified	Uncodified
Rigid	Flexible
Federal	Unitary
Constitutional sovereignty	Parliamentary sovereignty
Entrenched rights	Semi-entrenched rights
Separation of powers	Fusion of powers
Strong judiciary	Weak judiciary

Do you know?

1 What are the aims and principles of the Constitution?
2 How can the Constitution be amended?
3 How has federalism in the US changed?
4 How democratic is the US Constitution?
5 What are the similarities and differences between the US and UK constitutions?

4.2 Congress

You need to know

- the structure of Congress
- the shared and separate powers of each chamber
- the functions of Congress
- the effectiveness of Congress
- how congressional powers have changed

Structure of Congress

Overview

Congress is bicameral, made up of the House of Representatives and the Senate.

Table 69 Features of the House of Representatives and the Senate

Features of the House of Representatives	Features of the Senate
■ The House of Representatives has 435 members called 'representatives' ■ Each represents a district. ■ Representatives are allocated based on population. ■ Each state must have at least one representative. ■ Districts are reapportioned every 10 years. ■ Representatives are elected for 2-year terms. ■ They must be over 25. ■ They must have been a citizen for 7 years ■ They must reside in the state they represent. ■ In addition to the 435 full members, the House also has a number of non-voting representatives to speak on behalf of American territories.	■ The Senate has 100 members called 'senators'. ■ Each senator represents a state. ■ Each state has two senators, regardless of size. ■ Senators have 6-year terms. ■ They must be over 30. ■ They must have been a citizen for 9 years. ■ They must reside in the state they represent.

Synoptic link

The structure of Congress is set out in Article 1 of the Constitution. Any changes would require a constitutional amendment.

Key terms

Committee chair The chairperson of a committee who has power over the agenda and appointment of sub-committees.

Standing committee A permanent policy committee, often linked to a government department.

The committee system

Although major votes take place on the floor of each chamber, most of the real work is done in Congress's various committees, headed by powerful **committee chairs**.

Table 70 Key congressional committees

Committee	Definition	Membership	Key details
Standing committees	Linked to government departments on a specific policy area.	Senate: 18 House: 30–40	Determine whether or not to pass a Bill to the full chamber. Conduct investigations into its policy area. Hold hearings and determine whether or not to pass presidential nominees to the full chamber (Senate only).
The House Rules Committee	Determine rules regarding amendments to legislation and the order they are presented to the House.	13–15, House only	Allocate key rules: ■ open rules — unlimited amendments ■ modified rules — limits on the number of amendments, who can propose them and where they can go ■ closed rules — no amendments allowed
Conference committees	Ad hoc committees designed to reconcile differences between House and Senate versions of a piece of legislation.	Members come from each chamber	Agree a final version of a Bill. Once a final version of a Bill is agreed in a conference committee it will be sent back to each chamber for a final vote. If it is rejected by either chamber, it may be sent back to the conference committee or can be sent back to the original standing committee.
Select committees	Investigative committees for issues beyond one standing committee.	Various	Most are ad hoc, but there are five permanent select committees: Senate — Aging, Ethics, Indian affairs, Intelligence House — Intelligence

Congressional caucuses

Although dominated by the main parties, Congress is sub-divided into **congressional caucuses**. These are groups that meet with a shared goal or interest and can cross party lines.

Caucuses will:

- provide information to members on legislation and policy
- support each other in promoting a specific goal
- collaborate to promote an agenda

Key caucuses include:

- the Congressional Black Caucus
- the Congressional Hispanic Caucus
- the Congressional Hispanic Conference
- the House Freedom Caucus
- the Tuesday Group

Powers of Congress

Concurrent powers

- legislation: any law must pass both chambers
- power to investigate the executive branch
- overriding a presidential veto; must pass by 2/3 majority in both chambers
- initiating constitutional amendments — 2/3 majority in each chamber
- the impeachment process
- declaring war
- confirmation of an appointed vice president

Exclusive powers of the House

- beginning consideration of money Bills
- initiating an impeachment
- electing the president if there is no majority in the Electoral College

Exclusive powers of the Senate

- confirming presidential appointments to the cabinet, judiciary and ambassadorships
- ratifying treaties
- trying cases of impeachment
- electing the vice president if there is no majority in the Electoral College

Synoptic link

The US standing committees are similar to the UK's select committees.

Exam tip

As much of the work of Congress is done in committee, it will be important to reference them in any assessment of congressional power or effectiveness.

Key term

Congressional caucuses Discussion groups that meet to discuss a shared interest or concern. These can be party based, or bipartisan.

Functions of Congress

Representation

The frequency of elections, the growth in congressional primaries and the weakness of the US party system mean representatives and senators are much more engaged with their constituents than British MPs.

Representatives will engage with constituents by:
- holding 'town hall' meetings
- meeting with individual constituents
- making formal visits
- appearing on local media
- press interviews
- addressing popular groups

In representing constituents, representatives will:
- vote on legislation
- work on committees that deal with local interests
- help constituents with federal issues
- gain pork for their area through **pork barrel** policies

Factors that affect congressional voting include:
- **The 'folks back home':** constituent demands and needs.
- **The political party:** its ideology, position or assistance.
- **The administration:** the president may seek to persuade representatives.
- **Interest groups:** groups will lobby for beneficial legislation.
- **Colleagues:** senior colleagues will often advise or lobby others.
- **Staff:** congressional staff will give advice on legislation.
- **Personal beliefs:** some representatives follow their conscience.

Incumbent representatives tend to win re-election because they enjoy the following advantages:
- higher media profile
- a record on pork
- a favourable voting record
- party support
- an established war chest of funds
- support from key interest groups
- free franking privileges (free post) and support staff

Legislation

Legislation must go through the following stages in each chamber as shown in Table 71.

Synoptic link

The weakness of the US party systems gives constituents greater control over their representatives.

Exam tip

Whether representation in the US is effective depends on whether the trustee model (where representatives are entrusted to make decisions in the national interest) or delegate model (where representatives simply do as their constituents instruct) is preferred.

Key term

Pork barrel Describes funds given to benefit a congressional district.

Synoptic link

Voting records are publicised by interest groups to put pressure on a representative to vote the way their constituents want.

Exam tip

Different factors will carry greater weight depending on the issues, electoral cycle and the strength of the party.

Table 71 The legislative process

House		Senate	
Step	Can be defeated?	Step	Can be defeated?
Introduction of legislation	No	Introduction of legislation	No
Committee stage	At the mark-up stage At the final-vote stage	Committee stage	At the mark-up stage At the final-vote stage
Put on calendar by House Rules Committee	No	Put on calendar by unanimous consent	No
Debates and amendment of chamber	Vote on each amendment (back to committee) Vote to pass	Debates and amendment of chamber	Vote on each amendment (back to committee) Filibuster Vote to pass 2-day wait for recommittment
Budget and engrossment	No	Enrolment	No
Conference Committee		**President**	
Step	Can be defeated?	Step	Can be defeated?
Conference committee to resolve difference	No compomise reached Compromise can be rejected by either chamber	President signs into law	President can veto, which can only be overriden by two-third majorities in each chamber

Key term

Filibuster The process of using procedures and debates to delay business until a measure is dropped.

Exam tip

The legislative process has an inbuilt negative bias, meaning it is easier to stop a Bill than create a law.

Table 72 Differences in the legislative process

House	Senate
Speaker refers Bills to committee	Referral of Bills is easier to challenge
Discharge process	No discharge process
Timetabling by the House Rules Committee	Timetabling is agreed between the majority and minority leaders
All revenue Bills receive a second reading in the Committee of the Whole House	No such process
Limited debate	Unlimited debate (filibuster)
Rules on amendments	Fewer rules on amendments
Electronic voting	Personal voting
A tied vote is defeated	A tied vote is broken by the vice president

Key examples of legislation include:

- North American Free Trade Agreement (1993)
- No Child Left Behind Act (2002)
- Bipartisan Campaign Finance Reform Act (2002)

- Emergency Economic Stablizations Act (2008)
- Troubled Asset Relief Program (2008)
- Patient Protection and Affordable Care Act (2010)
- Wall Street Reform and Consumer Protection Act (2010)
- Tax Cuts and Jobs Act (2017)

Oversight

To scrutinise the work of the executive branch, Congress can:
- use the power of subpoena to gain access to documents and testimony
- hold individuals in contempt
- investigate and confirm presidential nominees
- appoint a special investigator

Much of the work of oversight is done by the standing committees. Members of the executive branch regularly have to attend questions from the relevant standing committee or a select committee

Congressional oversight is most effective when:
- there is divided government
- Congress is more popular than the president
- it is non-partisan

Criticism has emerged of oversight being used on a partisan basis to simply oppose the president, particularly with confirmations.

Congress can also oversee the Supreme Court by holding hearings and votes in the Senate on Supreme Court nominees and can bring impeachment cases against federal judges who fail in their duties.

Key terms

Subpoena A legal writ demanding that people are, or material is, presented to a body.

Non-partisan Non-partisan politicians do not allow party politics to effect their conduct.

Synoptic link

Unlike the Houses of Parliament, the executive has no formal presence in Congress, meaning Congress is freer to investigate the executive.

US/UK comparison

Table 73 A comparison of Parliament and Congress

Parliament	Congress
Bicameral (Commons and Lords)	Bicameral (House and Senate)
Executive is present	Executive is absent
Strong party discipline	Weak party discipline
Limited number of Bills introduced	Vast number of Bills introduced
Agenda set by the government	Congress sets its own agenda
Unequal powers	Equal power across the chambers
Sovereign	Bound by the Constitution
No approval of appointments	Approves some presidential nominees
Undemocratic elements	Democratic
Executive questioned by Commons	Executive members questioned by committee

Do you know?

1 What are the shared and separate powers of each chamber?
2 How is each chamber structured?
3 How is legislation passed?
4 What are the roles and functions of Congress?
5 How have the roles of Congress changed?
6 What are the factors that determine congressional voting?

4.3 The presidency

You need to know

- the constitutional powers of the president
- the informal powers of the president
- what the Cabinet and Executive Office of the President (EXOP) do
- why rivalries exist between EXOP and the Cabinet
- different theories of presidential power
- factors that can limit presidential powers

Constitutional powers of the president

The president has the formal power to:

- propose legislation
- submit an annual budget
- sign or veto legislation
- act as the chief executive
- nominate **executive branch** officials
- nominate federal judges
- to act as commander-in-chief
- negotiate treaties
- issue pardons
- to perform the duties of head of state

As head of government the president must oversee the day-to-day running of the federal government. As head of state, the president acts as a spokesperson and leader for the whole nation.

Key term

Executive branch The branch of government that takes action.

Synoptic link

In the USA the roles of head of government and head of state are combined in one person, but in the UK, they are separated between the monarch (head of state) and the prime minister (head of government).

Table 74 Examples of formal powers being used

President	Power	Detail
Clinton	Nominate federal judges	Ginsburg and Breyer
Clinton	Pardons	140 pardons on final day in office
Clinton	Commander-in-chief	Military strikes in Kosovo
Bush	Veto	Stem Cell Research Enhancement Act, 2005
Bush	Head of state	9/11 Attacks and Hurricane Katrina
Bush	Commander-in-chief	War on terror, Afghanistan, Iraq
Obama	Propose legislation	Patient Protection and Affordable Care Act, 2010
Obama	Nominate federal judges	Sotomayor, Kagin, Garland
Obama	Negotiate treaties	Trans-Pacific Partnership, Iran deal
Trump	Nominate federal judges	Gorsuch
Trump	Sign legislation	Tax Cuts and Jobs Act, 2017
Trump	Nominate executive branch official	DeVos, Tillerson, Kelly

Informal sources of presidential power

Electoral mandate

The president (along with the vice president) is the only office to be elected on a national basis. This gives the president greater authority when claiming to represent the nation and provide leadership.

The strength of the mandate depends on:
- winning a clear majority in the Electoral College
- winning the popular vote

The larger the Electoral College victory, the stronger a president's mandate.

A president who receives more than 50% of the popular vote has a stronger mandate.

A president who wins the Electoral College but loses the popular vote is seen to have a weaker mandate and carries less authority with the other branches.

> ### Key term
>
> **Electoral mandate** The authority given by winning an election.

Control over the executive branch

The president has the power to determine how laws are to be implemented, how funds are allocated, which cases to prosecute and has direct control powers to allow him/her to govern.

These direct controls include:

- **Executive orders:** legal documents instructing federal officials on how to carry out certain functions and what actions to take.
- **Signing statements:** a statement that some part of a law being signed by the president will not be enforced for constitutional reasons.
- **Recess appointments:** an appointment made to a federal office while the Senate is not in session. The appointment only lasts until the end of the following Senate session.
- **Executive agreements:** bilateral agreements with foreign nations that do not have the same status as formal treaties.

The Cabinet

Members of the Cabinet are appointed by the president to run a federal department.

Background of appointees

Cabinet appointees will usually come from:
- Congress
- state governorships
- big-city mayors
- academia
- the private sector related to their department

Cabinet posts are not elected offices but are confirmed by the Senate.

Presidents will often look to have a diverse Cabinet by having a mixture of people.

Factors considered when appointing a Cabinet:
- experience
- gender
- geography/race
- age
- ideology
- support
- bipartisanship

Cabinet meetings

While the main function of a Cabinet secretary is to run a department, the Cabinet will also meet, when the president chooses.

The role of Cabinet meetings:

- collegiality
- exchange information
- resolve disputes
- debate policy
- advise the president
- monitor Congress
- prompt action
- present a unified front

The role of Cabinet remains important, but its advisory role has largely been replaced by the Executive Office of the President EXOP.

Powers of persuasion

Due to the system of checks and balances, a successful president often needs to persuade the public, Congress, the Supreme Court or even their own Cabinet to their way of thinking.

> ## Key term
>
> **Powers of persuasion**
> The ability to persuade politicians or the public to support a point of view.

Table 75 **The power of persuasion**

In person	Perks	Other people
■ Personal meetings, phone calls etc. ■ Direct public appeals through the media ■ Claiming a popular mandate	■ Offering to support favoured legislation or projects ■ Offering federal spending (pork) ■ Personal visits or photo opportunities ■ Dinners at the White House ■ Playing golf	■ The vice president, through links with the Senate ■ The Office of Legislative Affairs, which lobbies Congress on behalf of the president ■ Cabinet heads of departments ■ Party leaders

The effectiveness of the power of president to persuade depends on:

- personal popularity
- strength of mandate
- the nature of the issues being discussed
- relationship with Congress
- party relationship

Executive Office of the President (EXOP)

The Executive Office of the President (EXOP) is the collective name for the heads of key executive agencies who advise and assist the president in running the executive branch. EXOP is based in the 'West Wing' of the White House.

EXOP was created and grew because:

- The role of the federal government had grown.
- The size and diversity of America had grown.
- The USA's international involvement had grown.

Table 76 The key EXOP departments

The White House Office (WHO)	The Office of Management and Budget (OMB)	The National Security Council (NSC)
■ Headed by the chief of staff ■ Organises the president's schedule ■ Grants access to the president (in person or through communications) ■ Gives public/press statements ■ Organises events	■ Advises the allocation of federal funds ■ Oversees federal spending ■ Approves executive policy proposals	■ Advises on foreign and military actions ■ Coordinates information from various departments and agencies ■ Can be used as an alternative to the State Department

Table 77 EXOP/Cabinet rivalries

EXOP	Cabinet
Physically close to the president in the West Wing	Scattered across Washington DC and the surrounding area
Regular meetings with the president	Ad hoc meetings (if any) with the president
Serves only the president	Serves the president and Congress, plus champions the department they head
Increased role in policy formulation	Marginalised role in policy formulation
Greater freedom from congressional oversight	Regular congressional oversight

Exam tip

The Cabinet is made up of departments, but EXOP is made up of agencies, offices and councils, which are less formal than departments.

The presidency

Table 78 Congress and the president can work together, or be hostile

Work together	Hostile
■ Make and enforce legislation ■ Finance the federal government ■ Staff federal offices and positions ■ Protect the USA	■ Reject a president's legislative proposals ■ Override presidential vetoes ■ Amend, delay or refuse to grant a budget ■ Limit war-making powers through the War Powers Act ■ Reject nominations ■ Investigate a president ■ Impeach a president

The Supreme Court needs the president to:

■ nominate federal justices
■ enforce its rulings

However, the Supreme Court can declare executive actions unconstitutional.

How effectively the branches of government work together depends on:

- the popularity of the president
- the size of the partisan gap in presidential approval
- the mandate of the president
- the party of the president
- the partisan make-up of Congress
- where they are within an electoral cycle
- the make-up of the Supreme Court
- the popular support or opposition towards key policies

Limitations on presidential power

While all presidents have the same constitutional powers, their ability to use these powers depends on a number of criteria.

> **Synoptic link**
>
> The factors affecting presidential power are similar in many ways to factors affecting prime ministerial power.

Table 79 **Factors affecting presidential power**

Factor	Detail
Electoral mandate	A stronger mandate makes it easier to persuade.
Public approval	Stronger approval makes it easier to persuade.
Congressional relationship	A supportive Congress is more likely to support a legislative agenda and confirm appointments. This is easier with unified government rather than divided government.
Composition of the Supreme Court	The Supreme Court may be more or less willing to strike down executive actions depending on its composition.
Term	Presidents become weaker as their terms progress, particularly in their second term.
Crises	Major crises can rally public and political support behind a president, making it easier to achieve his goals. However, a badly handled crisis can damage a president's reputation.

UK/US comparison

Table 80 **UK/US executives compared**

UK	US
Prime minister is head of government only.	President is head of state and head of government.
Powers are held by convention.	Powers are defined in the Constitution.
Prime minister has only one vote in the Cabinet.	The president is all powerful in the executive.
Cabinet is an important advisory body.	Cabinet is not an important source of advice.
Cabinet is appointed by the prime minister.	Cabinet is nominated by the president and confirmed by the Senate.
Members of the Cabinet must also be members of the legislative branch.	Members of the Cabinet cannot be members of the legislative branch.
The role of Cabinet has been undermined by the growth of the Downing Street machine.	The role of Cabinet has been undermined by the growth of EXOP.

Do you know?

1 What are the actual and implied powers of the president?

2 What is the role and effectiveness of the Cabinet?

3 What is the role and importance of EXOP?

4 How does presidential power vary depending on circumstances?

5 What are the limits placed on the president?

4.4 The US Supreme Court

You need to know

■ the structure of the federal judiciary

■ the power of judicial review

■ examples of the Court's work

■ the appointment processes

■ debates about judicial interpretation

Federal structure

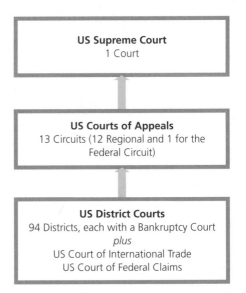

Figure 8 **The structure of the federal courts**

The Supreme Court is an appellate court, meaning it only hears cases appealed from lower courts and it only deals with constitutional matters. It is composed of nine members.

Independence

The Supreme Court is kept independent from the other branches because:

■ Justices have security of **tenure**.

■ Congress is constitutionally prohibited from reducing the justices' salaries.

■ The Supreme Court chooses which cases to hear.

■ Since 1935 it has been physically separated from the other branches.

■ Justices cannot also be members of the executive or legislative branches.

■ Since the 1950s, justices tend to be experienced judges or legal scholars.

However, independence of the Supreme Court has been challenged in recent years:

■ Candidates are appointed and confirmed based on political agendas.

■ There has been executive criticism of Court decisions.

■ The Court is being used by interest groups to change laws.

■ The Court has become increasingly involved in political debates.

■ *Bush* vs *Gore* (2000) directly involved the Court in the political process.

■ Many justices have worked in the political sphere or have clear connections to political parties (Roberts in the Reagan White House, Kagan in the Obama White House, Thomas is married to a political activist).

Judicial review

The Supreme Court's main power is that of **judicial review**. By this power, the Court can:

■ interpret the meaning of the Constitution

■ strike down government actions

■ strike down legislation

■ strike down state laws and actions

■ determine public policy

■ effectively amend the Constitution

■ effectively legislate

The power of judicial review is controversial because:

■ It is not expressly stated in the Constitution.

■ The Supreme Court granted itself this power in the cases of *Marbury* vs *Madison*, 1803 (federal law) and *Fletcher* vs *Peck*, 1810 (state law).

> ### Key terms
>
> **Tenure** Employment or time in office.
>
> **Judicial review** The power to review executive and legislative actions and declare them unconstitutional.

- It undermines the principle of a separation of powers.
- It gives too much power to unelected and unaccountable judges.
- It makes the Constitution too easy to amend.
- It can allow the Supreme Court to act as an all-powerful 'imperial judiciary'.

The appointment process

A vacancy must occur
A short list is drawn up based on advice from the Senate Judiciary Committee, White House Staff, the Justice Department and interest groups
Short-listed candidates are given FBI background checks
Candidates are interviewed by the president
Public announcement
Rating given by the ABA Standing Committee on the Federal Judiciary
Hearings are held by the Senate Judiciary Committee
The Senate Judiciary Committee votes on whether to recommend further action
Senate debates
A floor vote in the Senate

Figure 9 Process for appointing justices

Table 81 Strengths and weaknesses of the nomination process

Strengths	Weaknesses
Opportunity to scrutinise candidates	Politicisation by the president
Weak candidates can be pushed out before confirmation	Politicisation by the Senate
Candidates must cope with high pressure scrutiny	Politicisation by interest groups
Creates a degree of unanimity in confirmations	Politicisation by the media
Candidates have opportunities to express their thoughts and opinions	Politicisation along partisan lines

Synoptic link

The process for confirming Supreme Court justices in the UK is much less controversial because the UK Supreme Court is much less powerful.

The nomination process has become more politicised because of the growing importance of the Supreme Court. This is due to:
- the power of judicial review
- the increasing role of the Court
- the fact that justices have life tenure
- the fact that appointments occur infrequently

Candidate selection

When choosing a candidate, presidents will need to consider various important factors:

- judicial experience
- legal training and standing
- judicial philosophy
- diversity (race and gender mainly)
- the composition of the Senate
- the impact on the balance of the Court
- the opinion of key groups and supporters
- public opinion

Table 82 Current Supreme Court members with year of appointment

Conservative	Swing	Liberal
Chief Justice John Roberts (2005)	Anthony Kennedy (1988)	Ruth Bader-Ginsburg (1993)
Samuel Alito (2006)		Stephen Breyer (1994)
Clarence Thomas (1991)		Sonia Sotomayor (2009)
Neil Gorsuch (2017)		Elena Kagan (2010)

Key points:

- Apart from Kagan, the justices are all experienced judges.
- All went to Harvard or Yale Law School (6:3).
- Kennedy is the main swing vote.
- The liberal bloc is more unified than the conservative bloc.
- 4/9 clerked for a previous justice.

The Supreme Court and public policy

> **Key term**
>
> Public policy
> Governmental decisions that directly impact on society and the lives of the public.

Table 83 The impact of the Supreme Court on public policy

Public policy	Court decisions	Impact
Abortion	*Roe* vs *Wade*, 1973	Created a right to abortion
	Planned Parenthood vs *Casey*, 1992	'Undue burdens' could not be placed on a woman's right to choose
	Gonzales vs *Carhart*, 2007	Allowed a ban on partial birth abortions
	Whole Woman's Health vs *Hellerstedt*, 2016	Struck down state-based restrictions imposed on abortion clinics

▶

Public policy	Court decisions	Impact
Gay rights	*Bowers* vs *Hardwick*, 1986	Allowed states to criminalise homosexuality
	Lawrence vs *Texas*, 2003	Struck down laws criminalising homosexuality
	US vs *Windsor*, 2013	Struck down the Defense of Marriage Act (DOMA)
	Obergerfell vs *Hodges*, 2015	Extended the right to marry to homosexual couples
Affirmative action	*Regents of the University of California* vs *Bakke*, 1978	Allowed affirmative action, but not strict quotas
	Grutter vs *Bollinger*, 2003	Allowed race to be a factor in admissions, but not a set criterion
	Fisher v *University of Texas*, 2016	Upheld the principle of affirmative action
Voting rights	*Shelby County* vs *Holder*, 2013	Effectively struck down the Voting Rights Act
Healthcare	*NFIB* vs *Sibelius*, 2012	Upheld the right of the government to require citizens to have health care
	King vs *Burwell*, 2015	Upheld federal exchange programs
Elections	*Buckley* vs *Valeo*, 1976	Struck down restrictions on campaign spending
	Bush vs *Gore*, 2000	Ordered recounts in Florida to be stopped
	Citizens United vs *Federal Election Committee*, 2010	Struck down restrictions on private spending on elections
Immigration	*Arizona* vs *US*, 2012	Struck down Arizona ID laws
	Sessions vs *Morales-Santana*, 2017	Upheld the Trump travel ban, with some restrictions

Debates about the role of the Court

Table 84 Judicial activism and restraint

Judicial activism	Judicial restraint
Judges will involve themselves in public policy matters.	Judges defer to the other branches of government on public policy.
Judges ignore the principle of *stare decisis* or precedent.	Judges uphold *stare decisis*.
Judges promote an agenda.	Judges have no clear goals, other than the law.
Judges are willing strike down state and federal laws.	Judges are reluctant to strike down laws.
Judges are willing to strike down executive actions.	Judges tend to uphold executive actions.
Judges 'legislate from the bench'.	The Court restrains from 'legislating from the bench'.

Key terms

Judicial activism When judges make decisions to achieve a desired goal.

Judicial restraint When judges defer to other branches of government.

Stare decisis The principle that judges should consider past rulings.

Exam tip

An activist ruling can be conservative in nature or liberal. It is therefore possible to argue that the Roberts' Court has been activist in promoting a conservative agenda.

Table 85 Is the Supreme Court a political or judicial institution?

Political	Judicial
Judges are often appointed to fill a political agenda.	8/9 justices are experienced judges while the ninth is a respected legal scholar.
Justices are seen as conservative or liberal.	Typically, 75-80% of cases are unanimous or near unanimous.
Judges may be influenced by *amicus curiae* briefs from interest groups.	Justices have a high degree of legal training and experience.
Judges may be motivated by personal beliefs and external influences.	Court decisions can only be made based on the Constitution.
Court rulings may be activist.	Court rulings may be restrained.
Politicisation of the nomination process.	Security of tenure leaves judges free from political pressure.
Judges are increasingly being drawn into political debates about public policy.	The Court has to wait for a case to be brought before it can make a ruling (it cannot be activist).

Living constitution vs originalism

The living constitution theory believes that:

- The Constitution is open to interpretation through a loose constructionist interpretation.
- The framers kept it vague to allow it to evolve as the US changed.
- The role of the Supreme Court is to modernise the Constitution.

Originalists believe that:

- Like all laws, the Constitution is a dead document, not open to new interpretation, so a strict constructionist approach applies.
- Interpretations should be based on the original intention of the framers.
- The role of the Supreme Court is to apply the standard of 1788 to modern America.

UK/US Comparison

Table 86 Comparison of the UK and US Supreme Courts

UK	US
12 members	9 members
Nominated by an independent commission and confirmed by the monarch	Nominated by the president and confirmed by the Senate

Key terms

Political Suggests judges are motivated by a political agenda.

Judicial Judges are motivated only by the law.

Conservative A judge who makes decisions that promote a right-wing agenda.

Liberal Justices who are seen as making decisions that promote a more progressive or left-wing agenda.

Living constitution A theory that the US Constitution is living and therefore open to new interpretations and can evolve.

Originalism A theory that the Constitution is 'dead' and should only be considered by the original intention of the framers.

Strict/loose constructionist Strict constructionists stick closely to the words of the Constitution, while loose constructionists give greater interpretation to what is written, going beyond the words of the text.

UK	US
Small groups of justices hear each case	All justices hear all cases
Tenure until 75	Life tenure
Paid from an independent fund	Paid through Congress, but pay cannot be cut
Cannot overturn primary legislation	Can strike down any legislation or governmental action
Increasingly used in political issues	Increasingly used in political issues
Protects rights through the Human Rights Act (HRA)	Protects rights through the amendments
Cases can be appealed to the European Court of Human Rights or the European Court of Justice (for now)	There is no higher authority

Do you know?

1 How are justices appointed?
2 What are the criticisms of the appointment process?
3 What is the basis of judicial review?
4 How is the current court composed?
5 What are the issues relating to theories of judicial interpretation?

Key terms

Constitutional rights Rights that are protected by the Constitution.

Racial equality The idea of creating a level playing field between different racial groups, through equality of opportunity or equality of outcome.

4.5 Civil rights

You need to know

- key constitutional rights and where they are located
- examples of cases dealing with civil rights
- how voting rights have been upheld and infringed
- what affirmative action is and the arguments surrounding it
- how effectively minorities have been represented in the federal government
- the debates around immigration reform

Synoptic link

A strong understanding of the rights and Supreme Court cases relating to the Bill of Rights is essential here.

Rights protected by the Constitution

Many civil liberties, particularly those relating to **racial equality**, are protected by the Constitution, mostly under the Bill of Rights, with some later amendments also playing a role (notably the 13th and 14th).

Table 87 The Supreme Court and the Bill of Rights

Right (plus amendment)	Cases	Protection
Religion (I)	*Town of Greece* vs *Galloway*, 2014 *Burwell* vs *Hobby Lobby*, 2014	Reduced the separation of Church and state but argued to allow the free exercise of a person's religion.
Speech (I)	*Citizens United* vs *Federal Election Commission*, 2010 *McCutchen* vs *Federal Election Commission*	Extended conditional protections to corporations and groups, striking down restrictions on campaign spending.
To bear arms (II)	*District of Columbia* vs *Heller*, 2008 *McDonald* vs *City of Chicago*, 2010	Upheld the right of citizens to own handguns at home for defence.
Freedom from unreasonable searches and seizures (IV)	*Riley* vs *California*, 2014 *Carpenter* vs *US*, 2018	Protected digital devices from being searched or used without a warrant or due process.
To speedy and public trial by an impartial jury (VI)	*Boumediene* vs *Bush*, 2008	Protected the right of detainees held in Guantanamo Bay.
Freedom from cruel and unusual punishments (VIII)	*Roper* vs *Simmons*, 2005 *Baze* vs *Rees*, 2008 *Hall* vs *Florida*, 2014 *Glossip* vs *Gross*, 2015	Removed the death penalty for minors and those who are deemed mentally incompetent or disabled, but allows the principle of the death penalty under lethal injection to be continued.
Powers reserved to the states (X)	*US* vs *Lopez*, 1995 *Shelby County* vs *Holder*, 2013 *US* vs *Windsor*, 2013	Struck down federal restrictions on states.
	Arizona vs *US*, 2012 *McDonald* vs *City of Chicago*, 2010 *Obergerfell* vs *Hodges*, 2015	Struck down state laws.

Rights protected by other amendments

Table 88 The Supreme Court and other rights

Right (plus amendment)	Cases	Protection
Equal protection (XIV)	*Brown* vs *Board of Education of Topeka*, 1954	Struck down race-based segregation.
	Griswold vs *Connecticut*, 1965	Established a right to privacy.
	Obergerfell vs *Hodges*, 2015	Established homosexual equality.
	Fisher vs *University of Texas*, 2016	Confirmed the constitutionality of Affirmative Action Programs.
Gender equality (XIX)	*Ledbetter* vs *Goodyear*, 2007 *Wal-Mart Stores Inc* vs *Dukes*, 2011	Struck down company rules denying equality of payment, promotion or job assignments.
Voting rights (XV, XXIV and XXVI)	*Shelby County* vs *Holder*, 2013	Effectively struck down the Voting Rights Act.

Race and rights in contemporary US politics

Voting rights

Voting rights aimed to ensure the 15th Amendment was enforced in law and in spirit in all states and race could not be used to prevent people from voting.

Methods

Voting rights have traditionally been upheld more by Congress than the president.

The main tools were:

- the Voting Rights Act, 1965
- the Voting Rights Act Reauthorization, 2006

These Acts required areas with diverse populations and records of segregation to get approval from the Attorney General before making any changes to voting laws.

Attacks

- In *Shelby County* v. *Holder*, 2013, the Court struck down a key provision of the Voting Rights Act. As a result, nine states had introduced photo ID requirements by 2016.
- In 2017 the Supreme Court supported another lower court ruling striking down a restrictive North Carolina voter ID law.
- Voting rights are also restricted by **felony disenfranchisement**, with some states, notably Florida, banning anyone with a criminal conviction from ever voting again.
- An estimated 6 million African Americans have lost the right to vote as a result of felony disenfranchisement.
- Voter ID laws and felony disenfranchisement do not specifically restrict the right of minorities to vote, but they disproportionately impact on minority individuals who are less likely to hold or afford a valid ID and are much more likely to have been convicted.

Affirmative action

Over the years people have stated different aims for **affirmative action**. The key aims are:

- to develop a black middle class
- to provide black citizens with opportunities otherwise denied them

Exam tip

Not all the first ten amendments still have relevance today. Do not worry about learning all of them, just focus on the ones that have been the subject to major cases since 2005.

Key terms

Felony disenfranchisement Denying a person the right to vote based on criminal convictions.

Affirmative action A program of equality of outcome by which minority groups (usually African American) are given beneficial treatment; sometimes referred to as 'positive discrimination'.

Synoptic link

The arguments for and against allowing prisoners the right to vote are similar in the UK and USA, but there is a far greater racial dynamic in the USA.

■ to make up for past wrongs
■ to promote greater tolerance and diversity in society

Methods

Any attempt to give a benefit to a citizen from a racial minority based on their race is considered affirmative action.

The main areas of affirmative action have been:
■ busing (ruled unconstitutional)
■ quotas (ruled unconstitutional)
■ preferential consideration in college admissions
■ preferential consideration in school admissions
■ preferential consideration in employment and promotion

Table 89 Positives and negatives of affirmative action

Positives	Negatives
Increased minority admissions to college.	There are high rates of 'drop-outs' among those admitted via affirmative action.
It has created greater diversity.	It has led to race-based hostility from those who feel they have 'lost-out'.
It is justified by passed wrongs.	It perpetuates divisions based on race.
It has worked.	If it has worked it is no longer needed; if it is still needed, it does not work.
It is an effective means of creating racial diversity.	It does not go far enough in tackling racial problems in the USA.
It allows individuals to aspire and achieve.	It does not solve wider issues for minority communities. It undermines the achievements of successful minority citizens.
Key minority groups need it to create an equal place in society.	Other groups, like Asian Americans, have succeeded without affirmative action assistance.

Affirmative action and the Supreme Court

In repeated rulings, the Court has struck down strict quotas and benefits, but has defended the principle of race being used as a determining factor in admissions and employment.

However, dissenting opinions have been raised on the Court:
■ **Roberts:** 'the way to stop discrimination on the basis of race is to stop discriminating on the basis of race'.
■ **Alito:** 'affirmative action…based on offensive and unsupported stereotypes'.
■ **Thomas:** a recipient of affirmative action, he has been consistently critical of the effect it had on him of undermining his achievements.

Table 90 Has affirmative action been beneficial?

Yes	No
It has helped develop a black middle class.	It has caused division within the black community.
It has helped redress inequality in society.	It continues to perpetuate racial division.
It has led to an increase in minority admissions to higher education.	It has created a dependency culture.
It has helped minority citizens achieve higher positions in employment.	It has created resentment without benefiting all.

Exam tip

When considering whether affirmative action has been beneficial or not, think about who it may or may not be beneficial to; what benefits one group may adversely affect another.

Representation

Congressional

- Partly as a result of **gerrymandering** and minority-majority districts, representation of African Americans in the House of Representatives has grown since the 1960s.
- In the Senate, representation was generally much weaker, with Obama being only the third black Senator since the 1880s.
- The 115th Congress is the most racially diverse in history, and minority politicians now represent both parties in both chambers.

Key term

Gerrymandering The process of drawing district boundaries to benefit a particular party or disadvantage another.

Table 91 Minority representation in Congress after the 2016 elections

Group	House	Senate
African American	46	3
Hispanic	34	4
Asian	15	3

Executive

Table 92 Minority candidates seeking presidential nominations from major parties

African Americans	Hispanic
- Shirley Chisolm (D) 1972 - Jesse Jackson (D) 1984 + 88 - Barack Obama (D) 2008 +12 - Herman Cain (R) 2012 - Ben Carson (R) 2016	- Marco Rubio (R) 2016 - Ted Cruz (R) 2016

Synoptic link

The opening up of the presidential nomination process to minority candidates can be viewed as a positive of the primary process.

In the Cabinet there have been 20 African Americans in history. Most were appointed to lower-tier departments like Housing and Urban Development.

Recent senior appointments include:
- Colin Powell: secretary of state
- Condoleezza Rice: secretary of state
- Eric Holder: attorney general
- Loretta Lynch: attorney general

The Cabinet with the most number of African Americans was George W. Bush's first, while Obama's first Cabinet was the most racially diverse.

The Trump Cabinet is the least diverse in decades.

Supreme Court

As African Americans have traditionally struggled to access the high legal training needed to become a senior lawyer or judge, few have been in a position to be appointed to the Supreme Court.

Supreme Court justices have all been Caucasian with three exceptions:
- Thurgood Marshall
- Clarence Thomas
- Sonia Sotomayor

Immigration

- Hispanic immigration has become a major concern in American politics, focusing on issues over prevention of illegal immigration and what to do with the large number of illegal immigrants already living in the USA.
- Obama proposed the DREAM Act, but this was filibustered in the Senate.
- Obama issued an executive order, Deferred Action for Childhood Arrival (DACA), which ordered executive officials to grant citizenship to illegal immigrants brought over as children.
- Trump has repealed DACA, and wants to deport all illegal immigrants and build a wall to prevent further illegal immigration.

Key term

DREAM Act The Development, Relief and Education for Alien Minors Act.

Synoptic link

Obama's use of DACA and its repeal by Trump show both the strength and weakness of executive orders as a presidential power.

UK/US comparison

Table 93 UK/US comparison of rights protections

UK	US
Rights are mostly protected through the Supreme Court.	Rights are often protected by the Supreme Court.
Parliament and the prime minister also play meaningful roles in rights protection.	Congress and the executive can play a meaningful role in rights protection.
Rights are defined by common law and the Human Rights Act.	Rights are set out in the Constitution, mostly in the amendments.
Rights are not entrenched.	Rights are entrenched.
The Supreme Court has no power to strike down statute law or executive actions that breach the Human Rights Act.	The Supreme Court can strike down any law or action that breaches a constitutional right.
The Supreme Court has no power of enforcement.	The Supreme Court has no power of enforcement.
Rights protection has been growing since 2000.	Rights protections have been growing since the 1950s.

Do you know?

1 Give examples of cases dealing with civil rights.
2 How have voting rights been upheld and infringed?
3 What are the arguments surrounding affirmative action?
4 How effectively have minorities been represented in the federal government?
5 What are the different proposals to deal with immigration reform?

4.6 US elections

You need to know

- the constitutional requirements to become president
- the primary process
- the role of national party conventions
- debates about the workings and role of the Electoral College
- the role of incumbency of presidential elections
- the role of money in elections and attempts to regulate it

Presidential elections

Requirements

To become president, there are four constitutional requirements and many desirable non-constitutional qualities as outlined in Table 94.

Table 94 Constitutional requirements and non-constitutional qualities for becoming president

Constitutional	Non-constitutional
■ Be a natural-born citizen ■ Be 35 years old or over ■ Be resident for 14 years ■ Not to have served two previous terms	■ Experience of political office ■ The support of a major party ■ A positive image ■ Financial resources ■ A strong organisational structure ■ The right image for television, radio and social media ■ Relevant policies

The invisible primary

The period between candidates announcing their intention to run and the Iowa caucus is known as the invisible primary.

Candidates will attempt to raise funds, support and name recognition by:
- releasing books
- participating in televised debates
- holding rallies
- visiting early-voting states
- building a campaign team and offices
- developing a 'ground network' of supporters
- fundraising
- polling

The aim is to win the invisible primary by becoming the 'front runner' (the person with the most funds before the primaries begin).

However, winning the invisible primary does not guarantee the nomination. Winners of the invisible primary who did not go on to become the candidate include:
- Jeb Bush (R) 2016
- Hillary Clinton (D) 2008
- Rudi Giuliani (R) 2008
- Howard Dean (D) 2004

Primaries and caucuses

In primaries, members of the public are able to elect delegates to a party's national convention. These delegates will select the party's presidential candidate.

The primary process begins with the Iowa caucus, usually in January or February of an election year.

The party national committee determines the order and timings of state-based primary votes, but the rules and means of allocating delegates are left up to the party in each state.

State-based parties can choose to have:
- a primary vote or a caucus
- an open vote (meaning anyone can vote) or closed vote (meaning only registered party supporters can vote
- winner takes all (the plurality winner gets all the delegates) or proportional (some means of sharing out delegates based on voting outcomes)

Early primaries have a number of advantages, including:
- greater choice
- more media attention
- more influence with political figures
- more money spent in their state

Many states wish to gain an advantage by going earlier, which has led to states leapfrogging each other and made the whole process much longer.

National committees have imposed tighter rules to reduce the problem of **front-loading**.

Voter turnout in primaries is usually low, but it is determined by factors such as:
- the timing of the primary
- the type of primary
- whether it is a primary or caucus (caucuses are much lower because of the time commitments)
- who turns out (usually older, white and high income/education)
- the competitiveness of the contest
- whether or not the outcome has been decided

Key term

Front-loading The process of state party leaders trying to hold their primary earlier to gain an advantage.

Table 95 Positives and negatives of the primary process

Positive	Negative
Weakens the power of party bosses	Forces poor candidates on parties
More opportunity to participate	Low turnout
Greater scrutiny of candidates	Apathy from the electorate
Time to assess the candidates	Lengthens the electoral process
Greater voter choice	'Crazy' candidates
Candidates present themselves to the public	Expensive process
People get to know the candidates	Campaigns can become personal battles and populist

Proposals to improve the nomination process include:

- a national primary (all held on one day)
- a rotating regional primary (four super regions are allocated a month to hold primaries)
- a regional lottery primary (the order of regions is decided by lottery)
- back-loading (start with the smallest state and work through to the largest)

> **Exam tip**
>
> Most proposed reforms deal with the issue of front-loading and the length of the process.

National party conventions

Formal functions

National party conventions have three formal functions:

1 choosing a presidential candidate
2 choosing a vice presidential candidate
3 deciding the party platform

However, these functions are no longer very important because:

- candidates are chosen through the primaries
- presidential candidates now pick their vice presidential running-mates
- presidential candidates choose their own platform

> **Key term**
>
> **National party conventions** Meetings of party delegates held every 4 years to choose a presidential candidate for the party.

Informal functions

The informal functions of conventions have become increasingly important for election campaigns. These functions include:

- unifying the party after the primary campaigns
- enthusing the party base to campaign for the nominee
- winning over voters
- generating positive media reporting and a bounce in the opinion polls

The Electoral College

The **Electoral College** is a shadow congress with one job: to elect the president.

Electoral College votes are allocated based on:
- the number of seats a state has in the House of Representatives
- the number of senators a state has
- three Electoral College votes are awarded to Washington DC

There are 538 Electoral College votes in total and a successful candidate needs a clear majority to win: 270.

How the Electoral College works

- Voters elect delegates from their states, who have the job of choosing the president on their behalf.
- Nowadays many delegates are bound, meaning they have to vote the way the state has voted, but some will become a **rogue elector** and vote for someone else.
- Most states award all their Electoral College votes on a winner takes all basis, meaning a narrow win in a **swing state** can give a candidate all their delegates. For this reason, candidates can win the Electoral College without winning a majority of the popular vote.
- In Maine and Nebraska Electoral College votes are allocated by congressional district, with the state-wide winner of the popular vote gaining the two 'senate' votes.

> ## Key terms
>
> **Electoral College** The body that elects the president.
>
> **Rogue elector** An elector who does not vote for the candidate his/her state chose.
>
> **Swing states** States that could choose a candidate from either party.

> ## Synoptic link
>
> The Electoral College is set out in the Constitution, so any reform would require a constitutional amendment.

Table 96 Positives and negatives of the Electoral College

Positives	Negatives
It promotes federalism.	Large states are underrepresented.
It promotes a clear two-horse race.	It discriminates against third parties.
It enhances a presidential mandate.	It distorts the results.
It ensures national support for a candidate.	It is determined by a few swing states.
It usually works.	2000 and 2016 saw winners who lost the popular vote.

Possible reforms

Proposed reforms include:
- a national popular vote, but small states oppose this
- congressional district system, but gerrymandering means the wrong result is more likely
- a proportional system, but this would make a majority much harder to achieve
- getting ride of individual electors, but this would require a constitutional amendment

Factors affecting presidential elections

The winner of a presidential election is often determined by:

- the campaigns
- the incumbency factor
- media
- **campaign finance**

Campaigns

What campaigns need to do to be successful:

- enthuse the public to participate
- have an effective 'Get out the vote' strategy
- have a positive media presence
- target events and promotions in swing states
- raise sufficient funds
- perform well in debates

Incumbency

Primaries

Incumbent presidents rarely face a serious primary challenge. This means they can focus on fundraising and preparing for the election campaign itself, while their rival is being attacked by their own party.

Election campaigns

- Presidents have a record of achievement to be judged by.
- Presidents have had the opportunity to use federal pork in key states.
- Presidents gain higher media attention.
- If a crisis occurs, it gives the incumbent the chance to appear presidential by effectively dealing with it.

Media

How a candidate is portrayed by the media is crucial to success. Media can be either:

- earned, meaning press coverage that costs the candidate nothing
- bought, meaning paid for by the campaign, like adverts

Since the 1950s, television has dominated the debate, with political shows, presidential debates and adverts displaying a candidate's ideas and attacking opponents.

Since 2000, social media has grown in importance, with websites and viral videos promoting candidates and social media platforms like Twitter and Facebook allowing candidates to contact voters directly, generate earned media and shape the debate.

Campaign finance

Money is seen as essential in US elections because it funds:
- advertising
- staff and campaign teams
- travel
- support staff
- holding events
- polling

Attempts to regulate the amount of money being spent include:
- the Federal Election Campaign Act, 1974
- the creation of the Federal Election Commission to regulate elections, 1974
- the Bipartisan Campaign Finance Reform Act

These regulations were limited by Supreme Court rulings, which stated there could be no regulation on campaign spending.

Although the amount of money an official campaign can raise (**hard money**) can be regulated, the amount of money a private organisation spends campaigning cannot. This led to the creation of **super PACs**.

Impact of money

The cost of elections has increased dramatically since 2000. However, candidates and super PACs are usually well matched, so only in 2008 has money been a determining factor.

UK/US comparison

Table 97 A comparison of UK/US elections

UK	US
Elections are every 5 years, but can be earlier.	Congressional elections are every 2 years; presidential elections are every 4 years.
Election campaigns are usually 4–6 weeks.	Election campaigns can last up to 2 years.
Party leader is chosen by their party.	Candidates are chosen by the public.
Need majority support in the House of Commons.	Need a majority in the Electoral College.
Television advertising is banned.	Advertising is unrestricted.
Cost around £80 million in total.	Cost over $2 billion just for the presidency.
There are leadership debates.	There are presidential debates.

Key terms

Hard money The distinction between money that is not regulated (soft) and money that is regulated (hard).

Super PACs Organisations that can raise and spend unlimited amounts on campaigning if they have no direct coordination with the official campaign.

Synoptic link

Super PACs were established as a result of the Citizens United case, which ruled that corporations were covered by 1st Amendment freedoms.

Do you know?

1 How are the presidential candidates chosen?

2 How does the primary system work, and how could it be improved?

3 What is the importance of the party conventions?

4 Why are US elections so expensive, and why have attempts to regulate them failed?

5 What are the strengths and weaknesses of the Electoral College?

4.7 US parties

You need to know

■ how the main parties are structured
■ the core principles and policies of the Democrats and Republicans
■ intra-party factions
■ divisions within the main parties
■ which groups support which party and why

Party policies

Party structure

The main parties have a federal structure:

■ **National committees:** oversee the primary process, national policies and fundraising.
■ **Congressional leadership:** congressional leaders will develop policy and coordinate campaigns.
■ **State parties:** each state has its own version of the national party where candidate selection, delegate selection and local policies are carried out.

Democrats

The Democrats tend to:
■ hold progressive attitudes on social policy
■ favour greater government intervention
■ promote social welfare policies

Republicans

Republicans tend to:

- hold conservative attitudes on social policy
- favour limited government intervention
- protect American economic interests
- promote individual responsibility in welfare

Table 98 2016 party policies

Democrats	Republicans
Women should have the right to choose an abortion.	A foetus has the right to life.
Support for same-sex marriage.	Promotion of marriage between a man and a woman.
Reduce the impact of crime in minorities.	Support mandatory prison sentences.
Support for environmental measures.	Support fracking and the use of fossil fuels.
National minimum wage should be increased.	Minimum wage rates should be set at the state level.
All Bush era tax cuts to expire.	Expand Bush era tax cuts.
Support the Affordable Care Act.	Repeal the Affordable Care Act.

> ### Exam tip
> Divisions within the modern Democrat party tend to be over extent rather than fundamentals.

> ### Synoptic link
> Much like in the UK, American parties are divided into left-wing and right-wing factions.

Internal party conflicts

Table 99 Democrat factions

Policy	Moderate Democrats	Liberal Democrats
Trade	Free trade, support Trans-Pacific Partnership	Greater regulation of Wall Street
Education	Support for disadvantaged students	Free college education
Healthcare	Public private partnership in Affordable Care Act	Healthcare provision for all
Minimum wage	Increase federal minimum wage to $12 per hour	Increase federal minimum wage to $15 per hour
Military	Strong military and global role	Military cuts and limited intervention
Guns	Limited gun restrictions	Strong gun restrictions
Immigration	Immigration reform	Pathway to citizenship

> ### Key term
> Factions Groups that have different opinions within a party.

> ### Exam tip
> There are more fundamental divisions within the Republican party than just extent, explaining current problems for the party in Congress and between Congress and the president.

Table 100 Republican factions

Policy	Moderate Republicans	Social Conservatives	Fiscal Conservatives
Trade	Prioritise small businesses	Protectionism	Total free trade
Spending	Balanced budgets	Increases to military, defence and desirable social programs	Severe cuts to all areas
Welfare	Government safety net with individual responsibility	Individual responsibility	Reduce/eliminate federal welfare
Military	Support a strong military	Strong military and American intervention	Oppose military intervention
Immigration	Support for controlled immigration	Opposed to immigration	Favour immigration for jobs/oppose spending on immigration controls
Minimum wage	Reduce	Reduce	Abolish
Abortion	Opposed, except in some circumstances	Opposed in all circumstances	No strong position

Supporters

American parties are umbrella organisations that cover many different groups. This makes the national party a coalition of different groups, which may have similar or very different views on some issues.

Table 101 Typical party support among groups

Groups that tend to support Democrats	Groups that tend to support Republicans
Women	Men
Younger voters	Older voters
Racial minorities	White
Urban residents	Rural
Higher education (postgraduate)	Lower education (high school only)
Northeast and west coast	Central and southern USA
Low religious attendance	High religious attendance

Why groups vote as they do

Race

- Democrat support for civil rights legislation and action since the 1960s.
- Democrat support for affirmative action programs.
- High levels of poverty in minority groups increase support for Democrat welfare programs.

- Democrats have a higher degree of black representation.
- Democrat support for immigration reform.
- Republican opposition to affirmative action and civil rights legislation.
- Republican threats to 'build a wall' and deport illegal immigrants.

Religion

- Republican opposition to abortion laws.
- Appeals to the **religious right** by Reagan and George W. Bush.
- Democrat support for socially liberal policies that conflict with religious teachings.

Gender

- Republican opposition to the Equal Rights Amendment.
- Democrat support/Republican opposition to abortion.
- Democrat promotion of social welfare programs.
- Republican focus on military and conflict.

Education

- The lower educated tend to be lower earners and want Republican job protection.
- The lower educated tend to favour Republican pledges to curb immigration to protect jobs.
- Higher education has a liberalising effect.

> **Key term**
>
> **Religious right** People who support a conservative religious-based ideology.

> **Exam tip**
>
> Voting by groups refer to general trends and there will be many exceptions within each group. Coalitions of groups can also cause factions by having contradictory aims.

UK/US comparison

Table 102 Comparison of UK and US party politics

UK	US
Strong party control	Weak party
Two-party with multi-party elements	Two-party domination
Strong party unity	Weak party unity
Ideological cohesion	Coalition of factions
Limits on campaign activity	Almost no limits on campaign activity
Core role in contesting elections	Role undermined by candidates and super PACs
Centralised structure	Federal structure

Do you know?

1 How are the main parties structured?
2 What are the core principles and policies of the Democrats and Republicans?
3 What are the internal factions and divisions within each party?
4 Which groups support which party?
5 Why do key groups support a party?

4.8 US interest groups

You need to know

■ the role and significance of interest groups in American politics
■ what resources interest groups have
■ what methods interest groups employ
■ the impact of interest groups on democracy

Interest groups

Significance

Interest groups in the USA provide:

■ representation, in contrast to weak coalition/catch-all parties
■ participation, in organising social and activist campaigns for people to participate in
■ education, particularly **policy groups** in researching and publishing reports to support their positions
■ agenda building, as parties are less ideological, interest groups tend to set the political agenda
■ program monitoring, as interest groups will publicise voting records to ensure representatives vote as members wish

Resources

Pressure groups can play a major role in politics if they have:

■ a strong and activist membership
■ financial resources
■ policy expertise, particularly **single-interest groups**
■ a role in a specific sector, usually by **professional groups**
■ legal expertise

Key terms

Policy group A group that promotes a specific policy, e.g. the Heritage Foundation.

Single-interest group A group that promotes its own interests on a specific policy, e.g. the National Rifle Association.

Professional group A group that promotes the interests of a profession or interest, e.g. the American Medical Association.

Tactics

American interest groups use a number of tactics to achieve their goals, including:

- **Electioneering:** super PACs in particular spend vast sums campaigning on behalf of a favoured candidate.
- **Endorsement:** the public backing of a powerful group can help build support for a candidate.
- **Lobbying:** meeting with members to persuade them to follow a particular course or vote a particular way.
- **Advising:** meeting with members of Congress and giving them advice on how to vote and summarising Bills on their behalf.
- **Test cases:** interest groups may use the legal system to achieve their goals through bringing a case to the Supreme Court.
- **Organising activities:** interest groups organise protests and rallies, as well as persuading members of the public to contact representatives and protest outside institutions like the Supreme Court.

Table 103 The National Rifle Association (NRA) case study

Influence	Methods	Power
The NRA is able to persuade politicians not to adopt tighter gun regulation.	■ Legal challenges ■ Lobbying ■ Organising an activist membership to lobby	■ Most Americans favour the right to bear arms, so there are no strong countervailing forces to the NRA. ■ The NRA is able to prevent debate and discussion in Congress on even minor gun regulation, despite the rise of mass shootings.

Influence on government

Executive branch

To influence the executive branch, interest groups will:

- lobby members of the executive staff
- offer future employment for access through the 'revolving-door syndrome'
- maintain links and ties with executive departments, agencies and committees
- speak on behalf of the relevant agency in congressional committees
- assist in advice and implementation of policies

> **Synoptic links**
>
> The right to lobby is protected in the Constitution in the 1st Amendment under 'right to petition the government'.

Congress

To influence Congress, interest groups will:

- lobby members of Congress directly
- lobby congressional staff to arrange access

- lobby congressional committees
- provide evidence to congressional committees
- provide assistance to members of Congress
- organise constituents to lobby members of Congress
- publicise voting records to pressure candidates
- offer to support candidates

Supreme Court

To influence the Supreme Court, interest groups will:

- bring test cases
- lobby over nominations and confirmations
- organise protests outside the Court
- provide *amicus curiae* briefs

> ### Key term
>
> *Amicus curiae* briefs
> Friend of the court
> briefs provide advice and
> information to justices
> that may help them in
> understanding a case.

Influence on American democracy

Table 104 The influence of interest groups on American democracy

Positive influence	Negative influence
They provide information and assistance to promote better quality legislation and government action.	Information and assistance is in the interest groups' vested interest, not the national interest.
They aggregate views to help simplify complicated debates.	They oversimplify complicated issues.
They provide public education on key issues.	They manipulate the public on important issues.
They provide more effective representation than the parties.	They act in their own interest and are not accountable or well regulated.
They defend constitutional rights.	They prevent desirable outcomes from being achieved.
The scrutinise the work of elected officials.	They manipulate and hold power over elected officials.
They create opportunities for participation.	Direct action can be illegal and violent.

There is concern that super PACs undermine the role of parties in raising and spending vast amounts of money to elect favoured candidates. These candidates vote in accordance with super PAC issues rather than party policy and the public interest, weakening parties and undermining democracy.

UK/US comparison

Table 105 Comparison of UK/US interest groups

UK	US
Limited electioneering role	Strong electioneering role
Strong union presence	Weak union presence
Limitations on donations and spending	Very few limits on donations and spending
Difficulty of lobbying	Lobbying culture
Focus on the executive	All branches of government effective targets
Limited constitutional protection	Protection under the 1st Amendment
Usually weaker than political parties	Often stronger than political parties

Do you know?

1 What is the role of interest groups?

2 What is the power and influence of interest groups in the US?

3 How and why do interest groups target the different branches of federal government?

4 Assess the role of interest groups in American democracy.

End of section 4 questions

1 What are the main principles of the US Constitution?

2 What is federalism?

3 How is federalism upheld in the Constitution?

4 How effective is the Supreme Court at checking the other branches of government?

5 Why has the appointment of Supreme Court justices been criticised?

6 What powers are held by Congress?

7 Why is the Senate seen as more prestigious than the House?

8 Explain the negative bias of the legislative process.

9 How effective is Congress at checking the other branches of government?

10 What are the differences between EXOP and the Cabinet?

11 What is affirmative action and why has it been criticised?

12 Explain how minority representation has improved in recent years.

13 Why have voting rights laws been controversial?

14 Why is the electoral process so long in American politics?

15 What are the arguments for reforming the Electoral College.

16 Are the divisions within parties greater than the divisions between them?

17 Which groups of voters support the Democrats and why?

18 Which groups of voters support he Republicans and why?

19 How significant are interest groups in US politics?

20 To what extent do interest groups undermine democracy?